CHRISTMAS
Past

CHRISTMAS
Past

The Fascinating Stories Behind
Our Favorite Holiday's Traditions

BRIAN EARL

LYONS
PRESS

Essex, Connecticut

An imprint of Globe Pequot, the trade division of
The Rowman & Littlefield Publishing Group, Inc.
4501 Forbes Blvd., Ste. 200
Lanham, MD 20706
www.rowman.com

Distributed by NATIONAL BOOK NETWORK

page vi: "Posting a letter to Santa Claus," vintage etching circa late-19th century. © Gettyimages.com/picture
page vii: "Soldier on home leave at Christmas," illustration from the 19th century. © Gettyimages.com/clu

British Library Cataloguing in Publication Information available

Library of Congress Cataloging-in-Publication Data

Names: Earl, Brian, 1974- author.
Title: Christmas past : the fascinating stories behind our favorite holiday's traditions / Brian Earl.
Description: Essex, Connecticut : Lyons Press, 2023.
Identifiers: LCCN 2022024205 (print) | LCCN 2022024206 (ebook) | ISBN 9781493069392 (hardcover)
| ISBN 9781493069408 (epub)
Subjects: LCSH: Christmas—History. | Christmas—United States—History. | United States—Social life
and customs
Classification: LCC GT4985 .E17 2023 (print) | LCC GT4985 (ebook) | DDC 394.2663—dc23/
eng/20220623
LC record available at https://lccn.loc.gov/2022024205
LC ebook record available at https://lccn.loc.gov/2022024206

♾️™ The paper used in this publication meets the minimum requirements of American National Standard
for Information Sciences—Permanence of Paper for Printed Library Materials, ANSI/NISO Z39.48-1992.

For Dashiell,
a shining star upon the highest bough

CONTENTS

GETTY IMAGES

GETTY IMAGES

FOREWORD

Christmas is perhaps the world's most famous holiday—inescapable at stores, Starbucks, and streaming services for a good chunk of every year. Whether you can't get enough of the holiday cheer or start feeling fatigued before Thanksgiving turkey has even been served, you probably feel like you already know *a lot* about Christmas.

But even if you're one of those Christmas connoisseurs who can recite the lyrics of most holiday tunes and has a favorite fruitcake recipe that you share with friends each year, you might be surprised to learn that there's a lot more than meets the eye when it comes to many of our most familiar holiday traditions.

Customs that seem centuries old often turn out to be relatively modern inventions while seemingly recent trappings may have their own forgotten histories stretching back to the Victorian era or earlier. The beginnings of some of the most famous aspects of Christmas remain clouded in mystery or historical controversy, while others might have such rational explanations as to leave the holiday dreamer little recourse but to throw their hands up and exclaim, "bah, humbug!"
That is why *Christmas Past* is such a great addition to your holiday bookshelf, providing insightful, entertaining backstories of familiar traditions that will leave you appreciating the holiday that much more.

You could hardly find a better guide into these evergreen-scented origin stories than Brian Earl. Over the years, through his delightful podcast and writing, he has explored the holiday and all its nuances—whether nostalgic or modern, sweet or scandalous—and the fascinating aspects of our celebration of Christmas from all sorts of angles. Through every episode and post, Brian's love of all things Yule is apparent, and proves infectious. I've written two books myself about Christmas and its history and celebration, but come away from every conversation with Brian having learned something new and feeling more charmed by the way we honor this holiday than ever before.

I remember speaking with Brian for the first time years ago, when he invited me on to his podcast to share an unlikely Christmas story I'd uncovered about a huckster who used kids' Santa letters to enrich himself. I was struck by the way Brian was at once a no-nonsense researcher looking to get to the bottom of every story, and a holiday romantic. He was eager to delve into the sometimes dark past of Christmas, to uncover the facts behind the fantasy. But he always did so with an open-hearted sense of wonder about the characters, customs, and curious tidbits that make up the beloved holiday. It seems that the more Brian discovers about our Christmas past, the more deeply he appreciates those traditions—and that sense of excitement comes through in every page of this book.

Like a pile of enticingly wrapped presents under the tree, *Christmas Past* offers an embarrassment of goodies, each containing some wonderful surprises. At least a few of these chapters you may open quite sure you know just what you're getting, only to find they contain something delightfully unexpected—and which you'll want to share with family and friends at your soonest possible chance.

Alex Palmer, author of
The Santa Claus Man and *The Atlas of Christmas*

PREFACE

This book had two beginnings: the first with a wish fulfilled, the second with a wish denied.

I consider myself lucky to have experienced not only my earliest Christmases in the suburbs of Massachusetts but also to have done so during the 1970s and 80s. These two decades seemed to produce more than their fair share of popular culture, much of which became the stuff of Wish Book catalog pages and letters to Santa. My childhood Christmases were bedighted with Atari video-game cartridges, E.T. figures, Star Wars play sets, and a replica of Michael Jackson's jacket, which I still own. The other kids on the cul-de-sac would converge sometime on Christmas morning to show off Rubik's Cubes, Transformers, BMX bikes, Stretch Armstrongs, and Speak & Spells. And throughout the season, we'd dream and dream and dream of Tyco racetracks, Teddy Ruxpin, and Laser Tag. We'd look forward to the debut of *A Garfield Christmas Special* and *A Muppet Family Christmas.*

It was, in the parlance of the time, "totally awesome."

It would be pointless to tell you that I loved Christmas as a child. What child doesn't? But that particular brand of Christmas, the snowy New England kind in the 70s and 80s—yes, it was common to have snow on the ground at Christmastime back then, though things are different now—left a special kind of impression. It was made all the more special by growing up as one of five children in a large extended family and with a mother who loved Christmas more than anyone I've ever known.

The house would be bedecked with ornaments and decorations made at my mother's sewing machine and craft table: handmade personalized stockings, decorative Christmas soaps, and a felt Advent calendar, to name a few. The Hi-Fi was constantly on, playing compilation LPs put out by Grants and Goodyear, and featuring Christmas songs from the likes of Robert Goulet and Mahalia Jackson. The kitchen windows were perpetually steamed as anisette cookies and gingerbread baked, filling the house with wonderfully warm Christmas scents.

I can't pinpoint my first Christmas memory, but I can pinpoint my strongest. And this brings us to the "wish fulfilled" part of this book's origin. Many moments from those happy Christmas mornings are captured in photos that my mom took with her Kodak Ektralite 10 and later had developed at one of those drive-thru kiosks in the grocery store parking lot. The photos are the square kind with rounded corners, linen-texture finish, and guaranteed red eye.

In one photo, I'm sitting in an armchair on Christmas morning with a look on my face that's equal parts triumph and disbelief. My mom no doubt timed the snapshot for the exact moment my reaction registered. Sitting in my lap was a box labeled Chinese Illusions of Magic. It's your standard set of beginner's magic tricks for children, featuring linking rings, foam balls, and trick cards. But to me, it was the fulfillment of a wish more than a year in the making. I'd first seen it in the Service Merchandise Christmas catalog that arrived in the early fall, and was lured by copywriting promising "mysterious secrets of the conjurers—revealed at last!" I'd reread the catalog page over and over during the Christmas season and plan the magic shows I'd perform.

Magic is a common enough children's hobby (especially for boys), but there was another reason I'd taken an interest in it. Throughout the 70s and 80s I was entranced by prime-time specials from the likes of Doug Henning and David Copperfield, the kind that would replace regularly scheduled episodes of *CHiPs* and *Knots Landing*. I was hooked on magic, and determined to have Santa Claus bring me Chinese Illusions of Magic.

That Christmas, though, he did not. The secrets of the conjurers would have to remain unrevealed for the time being, and my disappointment was obvious.

But the following year Santa came through for me, and my mom made sure to hand me that gift last on Christmas morning as a climactic moment. It was a delay, not a denial. That magic set became one of the favorite possessions of my childhood and marked the Christmas where I not only became a child magician but also came to believe in the magic of Christmas in a way that I've carried with me all these years. Yes, there are many more photos tucked away in my mother's photo albums, ones I would have been too young to remember, or old enough to be embarrassed by. But this one moment sometime in the mid-80s is the one I always return to. It encapsulates for me all the things Christmas is: surprise and delight, anticipation and wish fulfillment, warmth and comfort, familial love, magic and enchantment, reminiscing and creating new memories, sights and sounds, scents and flavors, laughter and music, tradition and ritual, and, as the song describes, "tiny tots with their eyes all aglow."

This Christmas spirit has helped me escape the fate of some adults, who grumble at the first sight of Christmas items on the store shelves, who feel only the stresses and irritations of the Christmas season, and who vocally oppose the appearance of ugly Christmas sweaters and the Elf on the Shelf. (Though, truth be told, I can sympathize a bit with that last point.)

For me, the Christmas season has always been something to welcome early, celebrate fully, and prolong as far as social norms allow. And that brings us to the second part of this book's origin. It was sometime in early September 2015 when I found myself looking to get into the Christmas spirit. I had recently become an avid listener of podcasts from National Public Radio. Then, as now, I loved shows like *Planet Money*, *Freakonomics*, and *Radiolab*. These shows took everyday topics and made them feel fascinating and engaging with a unique style of storytelling that explores surprising histories and hidden connections. And on that September evening, I found myself searching my podcast app to see if such a style of podcast existed for Christmas.

Sadly, my search came up empty. In fact, at the time there were only a very small handful of Christmas-themed podcasts available at all. But my wish denied became the beginning of a journey that culminates in the words you're reading now. Because, in that moment, I decided to create the very podcast that I had failed to find.

I never set out specifically to start a podcast, only to create something that I thought ought to exist. I wanted to create a way of talking about Christmas where curiosity, fascination, and storytelling were front and center, where the things we experience season after season as a matter of routine are given new life, and where nostalgia and Christmas memories are there at every turn. I also had the gall to think that maybe I could contribute something new and original to Christmas: a program meant to mimic the style of public-radio news pieces, and delivered in the still-emerging medium of podcasting.

Christmas Past debuted in November 2016. Each short episode tells the story behind a familiar Christmas tradition, with the help of a leading subject matter expert. And each episode ends with a Christmas memory recorded and submitted by a listener. The concept was to get listeners into the spirit, tell an engaging story, tell them something they didn't already know, and re-create the feeling of reminiscing at a family gathering—all in the time it takes to wrap a few gifts or drive to the toy store.

No matter the topic, the approach is always the same: take a Christmas tradition, find a fascinating story behind it, and then find the leading expert to help me tell it. Over the years, I've tracked down curators, archivists, linguists, historians, biographers, farmers, botanists, CEOs, dancers, bartenders, chefs, postal inspectors, and professional Santa Clauses. You'll meet many of them in the chapters that follow.

The show has grown year after year, spurred by word-of-mouth recommendations, media coverage in *Vanity Fair*, *USA Today*, and the *Financial Times*, and live appearances around the San Francisco Bay Area, where I now live.

During the Christmas season I receive many wonderful letters and emails from listeners. One from 2021 comes to mind, where a listener wrote to tell me how she was grieving the loss of her cousin (her best friend), who had recently lost a two-year battle with brain cancer. The email went into great detail about how wonderful and talented and thoughtful her cousin was, how generous with her time she had been, how deep their bond was, and how much she had loved Christmas. As I continued reading, I learned about how the cousin had once orchestrated an elaborate Victorian-style Christmas celebration at a farm in her town, where all of her many creative skills in baking, musicianship, and decorating made it an event that people would remember for a lifetime. It was one of the few times I've ever been moved to tears from reading an email, and certainly the only time doing so from a complete stranger's message. The listener closed out the message by saying that listening to *Christmas Past* was providing a bit of comfort and joy to the dark days.

Messages like these aren't at all uncommon. I routinely hear from people who find comfort in *Christmas Past* after losing a loved one, or being displaced from their family or familiar surroundings, or simply going through a tough time. I hear about how an episode triggered a long-dormant Christmas memory, or that listening to the podcast feels like time spent with an old friend. While it's very flattering to receive these messages, it's also very humbling. For every time I've thought of abandoning the podcast (there have been a few) or cutting a corner to get an episode finished, I'm always reminded that *Christmas Past* isn't just about just me and my hobby project. It is a community of very special listeners all over the world to whom I feel deeply responsible to keep this unique Christmas celebration of ours going season after season.

The purpose of this book is the same as the one for starting *Christmas Past* back in 2016: to create something that I thought should exist. Yes, there are many books already about Christmas history, but none that approach the content the same way *Christmas Past* does. Here you'll find the fascinating stories behind 25 of our favorite holiday's traditions, presented in short chapters, with a secular viewpoint, and bolstered by the perspectives of experts from several disciplines. I wanted to deliver the *Christmas Past* experience in a new format, and make it available to a broader audience. (Even in 2022, the research tells us that large percentages of adults are not regular podcast listeners.)

My hope is that you'll find this book to be equal parts nerdy deep dive and warm-hearted celebration. In reading the story behind each Christmas tradition included here, I want you to share my deep love of, and fascination with, Christmas—and maybe even feel like a kid again.

May your days be merry and bright!

Willow Glen, California
February 2022

INTRODUCTION

Behind every Christmas tradition is a story—often, a forgotten one. Each year, as we string up lights, build a gingerbread house, and get ready for a visit from St. Nicholas, we're continuing generations-old narratives, while being largely unaware of their starting chapters. In other cases, we continue those narratives only in mention, rather than practice. Sugarplums, wassailing, and hot buttered rum, for example, live on in classic Christmas songs and literature, while remaining mostly absent from the typical modern celebration. Those narratives, by the way, are laden with fossilized language like "'tis," "'twas," and "humbug." Once common in speech and writing, these words seep into our collective vocabulary for only a few weeks a year and, as a result, have become almost exclusively associated with Christmas.

Still other traditions remain common elsewhere in the world, but never made it big here in America. The American Christmas owes a lot to the Brits, yet somehow, we've resisted adopting the Christmas pudding, Christmas crackers, and pantomime.

And we can consider ourselves lucky that many traditions barely even live on in mention, staying relegated to obscure or forgotten folklore, literature, and song. The Christmases of long ago were filled with superstitious rituals, monsters, threats of child abuse, and foods that we'd find positively stomach-turning nowadays.

The Christmas we celebrate season after season is a collection of traditions ancient and modern. It is not the complete collection, and it is not the final collection. It is merely a curated collection that best suits this moment in history and culture. Our familiar version of Christmas would be barely recognizable to our ancestors, just as Christmas in the far future will only vaguely resemble that of today.

For every Christmas tradition, there is the story of how it came into being. In some cases, there is also the story of how it transitioned from more common fare to an exclusive connection to Christmas. Eggnog and fruitcake, for instance, spent most of their existence as general items of celebration or indulgence. George Washington frequently served eggnog to visitors at Mount Vernon, while Queen Victoria served fruitcake at her wedding. Only in more recent times have they disappeared outside the Christmas season.

For many other traditions, there is the story of how it died out. A very literal and recent example of this happened when a fungal blight wiped out the American chestnut crop starting in the early 20th century. By the early 1950s, just a few short years after Mel Tormé (and Nat King Cole) immortalized the line, "Chestnuts roasting on an open fire," chestnuts had all but vanished from most people's Christmas celebrations.

It's worth pausing here to note that, strictly speaking, a tradition is a belief or practice passed from generation to generation. Not all things commonly called "Christmas traditions" fit this definition. However, this book uses the term in the colloquial sense of a practice associated with the Christmas season.

Historian Bruce David Forbes compares Christmas to a snowball. Roll a snowball, and three things happen. First, it grows larger as it accumulates snow. Second, it picks up pieces of anything else that lay in its path. And third, pieces periodically fall off as the mass of snow changes shape and buckles under its own weight. The Christmas we celebrate is an accumulation of many traditions from different cultures and different points in history. And that accumulation process is still underway.

For a celebration so steeped in tradition and folklore, and whose origins are so firmly planted in a millennia-old religious story, it's often surprising to realize just how malleable much of it is. It is constantly changing in ways large and small, fast and slow, permanent and impermanent. The modern era has only accelerated this process, as the world became smaller and more interconnected.

The Christmas we know and love today in America is only the latest of many iterations, and it's much newer than you may realize. The majority of what makes up our modern celebration was created in the last 150–175 years, and a great deal of the remainder isn't much older than that. You may be surprised to learn that Christmas wasn't a national holiday until nearly a century after the signing of the Declaration of Independence. Christmas trees didn't start appearing in American homes until the 1850s, and weren't especially common until decades later. Many banks and schools were open on Christmas Day well into the early 20th century.

While the Brits of the Victorian Era began this most recent iteration of Christmas, America put on the finishing touches, and today wields the greatest cultural influence over it. The Victorians can take credit for "domesticating" Christmas. Previously, the celebration had been a public one, akin to Mardi Gras or New Year's Eve, for communities to celebrate in the pubs and the streets, as opposed to one for families to celebrate in the home. Victorian literature, especially Charles Dickens's *A Christmas Carol*, were hugely influential in shaping our notion of the holiday.

But only in America could Christmas have evolved and synthesized as quickly and dramatically as it did. Despite a 17th-century puritanical ban on Christmas in the Massachusetts Bay Colony, the transition from the 18th to 19th centuries marked a period of rapid change and growth.

The mingling of diverse immigrant traditions created a melting pot of Christmas cheer: the Germans with their decorated fir trees, the Dutch with their Sinterklaas legend, Scandinavians with their wreaths hung on the front door. The economy was transitioning from largely agricultural to industrial, with store-bought items becoming more a part of everyday life, and with increasing wealth to buy them. Merchants sought new markets for the influx of goods, nudging Christmas ever further toward being a major commercial and gift-giving event. And helping all of this along was a print media boom, which presented an ability to influence how people understand and experience Christmas, as well as a new avenue for businesses to reach potential customers.

New York City became (and largely remains) America's Christmas cultural epicenter, introducing the first commercial Christmas-tree lot, large store window displays, the first public Christmas-tree display, and the first home to display electric Christmas lights. Soon after, it became home to the annual Macy's Thanksgiving Day Parade, marking what we collectively recognize as the beginning of the Christmas season. (Yes, even the length of the Christmas season itself, the five-week period leading up to Christmas Day, is a very new and mostly contrived concept.)

Our changing world helped shape Christmas, and Christmas in turn helped shape our changing world. As we become a more commercial culture, for instance, so too does Christmas become more commercial, which in turn creates new opportunities for commerce. The historian Stephen Nissenbaum describes Christmas as not only a reflection of our changing culture, but also one of the forces driving that change. It is both a cause and an effect. Christmas, then, serves as a useful lens through which to examine our culture's attitudes toward materialism, religion, charity, tradition, fellowship, and much more.

Christmas is many things. It can be magical, stressful, sentimental, crassly commercial, overbearing, joyous, nostalgic, repetitive, and strange. And all of that makes Christmas endlessly fascinating. Knowing the stories behind some of our favorite holiday's traditions adds a new level of depth to our Christmas spirit (not to mention a handful of anecdotes to share at Christmas parties). This book includes 25 such stories. It's a festive, digestible Advent calendar of a book. Covering traditions ancient and modern, here you'll find stories of happy accidents, cultural histories, criminal capers, and hidden connections between Christmas and broader social, economic, and technological influences.

How did the invention of plate glass forever change the Christmas season? What common Christmas item helped introduce fine art to the masses? Why do Americans typically spike their eggnog with rum, rather than the traditional brandy? And speaking of booze, does using the phrase "Merry Christmas" mark you as a drunken reveler? You're about to find out the answers to these questions, and many more.

A Note on the Text

Each chapter in this book features commentary from subject matter experts in various fields and disciplines. All of the quotes included here are taken from interviews conducted by the author between 2016 and 2021 for the *Christmas Past* podcast.

PART I

What would Christmas be without those once-a-year flavors, filled with winter spices and sweet memories? Traditional food and drink help to make the season bright, as well as fascinating. Just what the heck is a sugarplum, anyway? And what do they have to do with hush money? Why does everyone hate fruitcake all of a sudden? Why do we spike our eggnog with rum? Can mince pies give you nightmares? Read on to find out.

CHAPTER 1

SUGARPLUMS

Nothing Says "Merry Christmas" Like Hush Money

Try to imagine a Christmas where you don't hear about sugarplums. Or try to imagine sugarplums without thinking of Christmas. Or, come to think of it, try to imagine a sugarplum.

What comes to mind? Plums with sugar on them? Some sugary treat in the shape of a plum? Well, it's neither of those. And isn't it strange that this thing that's so familiar to all of us in some way, something you've probably heard about every year since birth, is also almost completely unknown?

You have almost certainly never seen or tasted a real sugarplum. Nowadays, sugarplums and Christmas go together like rum and eggnog. But of course, it wasn't always that way. The backstory is as full of surprises as a stocking hung by the chimney with care.

For most of us, our first visions of sugarplums came from Clement Clarke Moore's "A Visit from St. Nicholas," a poem now generally known as "'Twas the Night Before Christmas." But what, exactly, is supposed to be dancing in our heads?

Did You Know?

Sugarplum is a common name for some plants, including Amelanchier canadensis *(aka bilberry) and* Diospyros virginiana *(aka American persimmon).*

The first time the world heard of sugarplums was in a pamphlet published in England in 1608. The author wasn't talking about sugarplums as a kind of candy, or having anything to do with Christmas: He used the word to describe a bribe given to keep someone quiet. No one knows for sure where the term came from, or to what it actually referred—possibly fruit preserved in sugar, which was a fairly new idea back in the 17th century.

We had the word before we had the sweet, but about 50 years later, the term had already fallen into general usage and was a common phrase used to describe these candy-coated nuts and seeds known as comfits. Interestingly, the word "comfit" comes from the Latin *conficere*, which means "to make." It's also where we get the words "confection" and "confetti."

Ask Your Doctor If Sugarplums Are Right for You

Comfits were usually caraway seeds or fennel or cardamom pods, and typically they were sold as remedies for indigestion and bad breath. In fact, you could only get them at apothecaries, and even then, only if you had a lot of money. Sugar was really expensive back then, not like it is now, where you can buy a bag at the store for a buck or two. And making comfits was delicate work, something that only a trained and skilled confectioner could do.

Entered according to Act of Congress, in the year 1868, by the United States Confection Company, in the Clerk's Office of the District Court of the United States for the Southern District of New York.

Product label for Santa Claus Sugar Plums. WIKIMEDIA COMMONS

Eventually, of course, the price of sugar fell dramatically, and new industrial processes were invented that allowed for sugarplums to be produced in large quantities. That meant more sugarplums on the market and more people who could afford them, and it wasn't long before people noticed that, in addition to being a useful remedy, these things just tasted good. Eventually, they moved from the apothecary to the confectioner's counter, and confectioners would sell them in cones and would color them red and yellow and green.

So "sugarplum" begins its life as slang for a bribe before being used to describe candy-coated nuts and seeds, but there's another phase yet to come: Later, people began using "sugarplum" to describe anything sweet, whether literally or figuratively, and sometimes it was even just shortened to just "plum." That explains why, to this day, we describe a cushy job as a "plum position," or why plum pudding doesn't actually contain plums. It also explains why Tchaikovsky made the Sugar Plum Fairy the ruler of the land of sweets in *The Nutcracker* (see Chapter 11).

PHOTOFEST

Eugene Field was a 19th-century poet known as "the poet of childhood." Those visions of sugar-plums dancing in the heads of the children in "A Visit From Saint Nicholas" just may have looked something like the magical world described in Field's poem, "The Sugar-Plum Tree."

THE SUGAR-PLUM TREE

Have you ever heard of the Sugar-Plum Tree?
'Tis a marvel of great renown!
It blooms on the shore of the Lollypop sea
In the garden of Shut-Eye Town;
The fruit that it bears is so wondrously sweet
(As those who have tasted it say)
That good little children have only to eat
Of that fruit to be happy next day.

When you've got to the tree, you would have a hard time
To capture the fruit which I sing;
The tree is so tall that no person could climb
To the boughs where the sugar-plums swing!
But up in that tree sits a chocolate cat,
And a gingerbread dog prowls below—
And this is the way you contrive to get at
Those sugar-plums tempting you so:

You say but the word to that gingerbread dog
And he barks with such terrible zest
That the chocolate cat is at once all agog,
As her swelling proportions attest.
And the chocolate cat goes cavorting around
From this leafy limb unto that,
And the sugar-plums tumble, of course, to the ground—
Hurrah for that chocolate cat!

There are marshmallows, gumdrops, and peppermint canes,
With stripings of scarlet or gold,
And you carry away of the treasure that rains,
As much as your apron can hold!

So come, little child, cuddle closer to me
In your dainty white nightcap and gown,
And I'll rock you away to that Sugar-Plum Tree
In the garden of Shut-Eye Town.

As those children were nestled all snug in their beds, those visions dancing through their heads could have been actual sugarplums. But it also could have been a metaphor for sweet dreams in general. We'll never know for certain, but what we can definitely say is that Christmas and sugarplums are connected the way that they are specifically because they were mentioned in both "A Visit from St. Nicholas" and *The Nutcracker*. Both were written in the 1800s, when the word "sugarplum" was at the peak of its popularity.

Sugarplums have been revamped for the modern age, and if you Google around, you'll find no shortage of recipes. Most of them are variations on the basic idea of taking some kind of dried fruit and nuts, putting them in a food processor along with some spices and sweetener until it forms a thick and sticky paste, and then rolling it into small balls and dusting them with sugar. Of course, these bear no resemblance at all to traditional sugarplums, but so what? They're easy to make, and a real crowd-pleaser.

CHAPTER 2

MINCE PIES

"Where's the Beef?"

In 1909, the *Trenton Evening Times* newspaper reported on a strange and tragic occurrence involving one Albert Allen of Chicago and his wife, who was found shot in the head, a gunshot wound from Albert Allen's gun.

Now, if you've ever read a detective novel or watched an episode of *Law & Order*, you know that when investigating a suspect, you're looking for three things—the means, motive, and opportunity. Albert Allen certainly had the opportunity. He and his wife lived together, naturally, and she was shot while she slept. He had the means because he owned a gun. But did he have a motive? Well, not exactly. According to Albert Allen, the mince pies made him do it.

The newspaper quoted him as saying, "I ate three pieces of mince pie at 11:00 and got to dreaming that I was shaking dice. The other fellow was cheating, and I tried to shoot his fingers off. When I awoke, I was holding a pistol in my hand, and my wife was shot."

And if you think that's weird, well, we're just getting warmed up. Because the mince pie is one of the least understood, most maligned, and sometimes subversive Christmas traditions we have. And yet it's still here, with its pastry crust, spiced and often boozy fruit filling. It's a survivor, and its story touches on hallucinogens, Prohibition, food preservation, the Puritans, and a Christmas dessert with a bad-boy reputation, a dessert that's as American as . . . well, as American as mince pie.

Mince Meat with the tang of Apple Cider

By a rich and rare old recipe is Libby's Mince Meat made.

First come the apples—luscious fruit picked when juicy ripe.

Then flaky white suet and choice cuts of meat chopped fine.

Then currants from Greece; and raisins sweetened full in California's sunshine.

Cinnamon, nutmeg and cloves, fragrant spices of the Orient.

And brown sugar to candy the other fruits—citron, orange and lemon.

"Enough," you say. No, not enough for this rare old recipe of Libby's.

There's that finishing touch—pure apple cider well boiled down!

To the far corners of the world we've gone for these ingredients. And Libby's chefs have mixed them with the skill for which they're famed.

Libby's Mince Meat—ready for your Thanksgiving pies! You'll want to add not a single thing, so rich and moist it is with its own sweet juices.

Get it from your grocer now—in glass jars, in tins or in bulk from the sanitary container. You'll find it inexpensive; you'll find it wonderfully good.

Libby's Mince Meat with the tang of Apple Cider!

Libby, McNeill & Libby, 511 Welfare Bldg., Chicago

Libby, McNeill & Libby of Canada, Ltd., Chatham, Ont., Canada

An 1839 advertisement appearing in the Saturday Evening Post. Packaged mincemeat filling was a common store-bought item, which became even more popular during Prohibition! WIKIMEDIA COMMONS

What, Exactly, Is Mincemeat?

Given the amount of labor and time that goes into making homemade mincemeat—it's recommended that you seal up and store your pie filling for a month or so before you put it into a crust and bake it—most people buy their mincemeat in a jar without thinking too much about the specifics of the ingredients. But there are no hard-and-fast rules about the contents of mincemeat, as you discover when you begin comparing recipes.

Novelist Jeanette Winterson says the packaged kind is always too dry and definitely needs more booze, but her homemade recipe includes apples, suet, sultanas (Americans call these "golden raisins"), currants, raisins, raw sugar, almonds, lemon juice, nutmeg, cinnamon, and brandy. "You can add candied peel if you like it," she writes in her collection Christmas Days. *"I hate it."*

Martha Stewart does like the candied peel—she includes candied orange and lemon rind in hers, along with the zest and juice of both fruits—along with apples, apricots, dried red plums, golden raisins, Medjool dates, brown sugar, cinnamon, cardamom, and cognac. No suet for her, although she does put lard in the pie crust.

Nigella Lawson offers up a "Cranberry Studded Mincemeat" in her holiday cookbook Nigella Christmas. *"It tastes both rich and boozy and fresh and fruity at the same time," she writes, "and it makes for a slightly different mince pie, but in a welcome rather than challenging way." Her take on this traditional favorite features both fresh and dried cranberries, currants, raisins, the juice and zest of one clementine, honey, brown sugar, cinnamon, ginger, cloves, almond and vanilla extracts, and both ruby port and brandy.*

Julia Moskin of the New York Times *blends an apple, dried figs, pecan halves, dried cherries, golden raisins, butter, brown sugar, ginger, nutmeg, allspice, clove, the juice and zest of one lemon, and brandy.*

And if all of this sounds too complicated, the legendary Julia Child once recommended a method to "spiffy up" store-bought mincemeat by adding freshly grated apple and a little liquor, and then heating it up on the stove.

There's a poem from 1573 (see Chapter 5) that describes the ideal Christmas dinner, and in it, the poet refers to "shred pie." These were made of various kinds of shredded meat and included dried fruit like currants, raisins, and dates, as well as spices. These shred pies—which were also sometimes known as "mutton pies" and would later be renamed "mince pies"—didn't start out as strictly Christmas fare.

According to journalist Veronique Greenwood, who has written about mince pies for the BBC, "The general idea of mince pies being a sweet, fruity, kind of boozy—sometimes, maybe a bit of meat at the beginning—is pretty old. It definitely predates the association of mince pies with Christmas. By the time you get to [the turn of the 18th century], mince pies do seem to be a sort of a winter thing."

But the transformation from everyday pie to winter and Christmas pie, as well as the rebranding from shred pie to mince pie, aren't the most dramatic changes in its evolution.

"It is striking," notes Greenwood, "that all the recipes at the beginning read 'you take your ground,' meaning you take a bag full of meat—well, now there's no meat."

To understand how this happened, you need to forget what you know about pies for a moment. Nowadays, we have our two basic kinds—sweet and savory. They're either filled with some kind of fruit or custard or meat; they're usually wide and shallow and have some kind of pastry crust on the bottom and sometimes, but not always, a crust on top, too. And nowadays, the crust and the spices and the flavoring are all meant to be part of the texture and flavor. But all of that is comparatively new.

Says Greenwood: "If you're interested in reading old cookbooks, you eventually start to notice all these recipes for things that they're calling pies. The crust doesn't sound all that good; it's just water and flour. And eventually maybe there's some lard, but it becomes clear that initially, pie crusts were thought of as a preservation tool. You would make this thick layer of dough, and line a pan, and then you would fill it with something—usually meat—and then you would bake it until it was hard. And you would pour in, through the steam hole that you had cut in the top crust, some liquid fat, and when it solidified, was airtight."

More Sweet, Less Meat

Dried fruits and spices were as much about preservation as they were about flavor. And they were the go-to until another commodity with similar preservative qualities became much cheaper and more widely available—sugar. From there, the meat was gradually phased out in favor of a purely dessert-like spiced fruit pie.

"By 1747, which is when Hannah Glass wrote *The Art of Cookery*—which is a really useful tool if you're looking to understand the evolution of English cookery—she describes how to make a mince pie," Greenwood continues, "and she doesn't actually mention meat until the end. She says you take currants, raisins, suet, sugar, lemon, orange peel, red wine, you make this mixture. And then she says, 'If you choose meat in your pies, parboil a neat tongue, peel it and chop the meat as finely as possible.' You don't have to put meat in this pie. It can just be sweet.

"By 1861, *Mrs. Beeton's Book of Household Management*, which is another really useful source, has a sweet, meat-free recipe and a meat recipe. You can choose which one you want. Twenty years later, by the Victorian era, it was kind of uniformly sweet."

The fact that mince pies made it into a 1747 cookbook at all is an achievement in itself—or at least that's a popular interpretation of events. Because back in the previous centuries, when England was under Oliver Cromwell's puritanical government, all things Christmas were quashed. Christmas celebrations were closely associated with Catholicism as far as the Puritans were concerned, and maybe you've even heard the common assertion that mince pies in particular, were made illegal.

Says Greenwood, "There's quite a lot of pretty fanciful articles and blog posts out there saying that mince pies were made illegal during the time of Oliver Cromwell, and those laws have never been repealed, so mince pies are technically illegal. But the more I read and the more I actually tried to figure out, 'OK, but which laws are we talking about?' the more I realized that it's just not true."

Did You Know?

The contents of a mince pie were said to symbolize the gifts of the Magi. At Christmastime, the pie was commonly made in an oblong shape to resemble a crib.

"What is true is that the Puritans were anti-Christmas, but they didn't actually make mince pies illegal. That idea appears to date from some later works from people who had an incentive to paint the Puritans as kind of ridiculous."

But plenty of people would ridicule mince pies, too. That would happen here in America in the 19th and early 20th centuries. Here's the interesting thing: Before apple pie was considered the one true American pie, mince pie held that title. It was eaten during the holiday season, of course, but also year-round, and it was part of the national identity. According to some, developing a taste for mince pie was proof of assimilation to American culture for immigrants. It was a morale booster and a comforting taste of home sent to American Expeditionary Forces in World War One. Its popularity and longevity are surprising, given that it was commonly thought to cause severe indigestion, hallucinations, and vivid nightmares.

In an issue of the *Woman's Home Companion*, one article states that "positively no stomach can digest mince pie without injury, and no intelligent woman in these enlightened times serves it to her family." There were newspaper cartoon strips mocking mince pies. One sermon described them as "very white and indigestible upon the top, very moist and indigestible at the bottom, with

Panels from the 1936 comic strip Keeping up with the Joneses. LIBRARY OF CONGRESS

untold horrors in between." There were recommendations to eat sand from the shores of Lake Michigan to prepare the stomach for eating them. It goes on and on, and probably by now helps you to understand why Albert Allen would say the strange effects of eating mince pie were to blame for him shooting his wife.

Bartender, Fetch Me Some Pie Filling

We had a love-hate relationship with mince pie here in America. But that pendulum swung more toward love in 1919, because of a little thing known as Prohibition. Greenwood observes, "During Prohibition—a time, of course, when many people were looking for ways to get alcohol in ways that weren't technically illegal—canned mince pie filling was a good candidate. The canned mince pie samples had an alcohol content of 14.12%; that's basically the same as wine. If you ate a can of this pie filling, you would probably feel pretty buzzed."

And here we are about a century later. The phrase "American as apple pie" caught on sometime in the 1940s, and mince pie was demoted to a strictly seasonal dessert—and a second-tier one at that. Today, they're much more popular in England, Australia, and New Zealand. In America, they've by and large fallen into the same category as fruitcake (see Chapter 3), which is to say, an acquired taste.

But love it or hate it, mince pie is intricately woven into food history, American history, and Christmas history.

CHAPTER 3

FRUITCAKE

Haters Gonna Hate

Every year, shortly after Christmas, the town of Manitou Springs, Colorado, hosts a raucous event known as a "fruitcake toss." It all started back in 1996, when a group of locals faced an all-too-familiar problem: It's early January, and the holiday season is officially over. The decorations have been taken down and stored, and the leftovers have all been eaten. Yet one item remains untouched, unwanted and, to many, unpalatable: that dense, sticky fruitcake with its neon green and red cherries and alcohol-infused flavor. So sweet, it makes your teeth ache just by looking at it. And where did it even come from? Maybe someone brought it along to a party. Maybe old Auntie Agnes sent it in the mail. Maybe it came as a gift package from an old acquaintance. But one way or another, it's gotta go.

And the only fitting way to get rid of a dessert you can't stand is not to throw it *away*, but to throw it as *far* as you possibly can. So, locals and curiosity seekers alike gather on January 3 in an open field to see who can throw a fruitcake the farthest. Or, as some attendees in Manitou Springs manage, catapult or slingshot or cannon-blast it the farthest.

How did we get here? Fruitcake is steeped in history and tradition, tied closely to the Christmas celebration, and often soaked in booze, no less. When and how did it go on to become so widely mocked? What made it the butt of so many jokes and shot from so many catapults?

Fruitcake: The Original Energy Bar

The earliest form of fruitcake goes back to the ancient Romans, though their version bore little resemblance to what we know today. They combined barley mash, pomegranate seeds, raisins, and pine nuts, and mix it all up and shape it into "cakes"; the result was more like what we'd now think of as an energy bar, a portable source of calories with a long shelf life. In fact, Roman soldiers would take these with them into battle.

The actual word "fruitcake" goes back to the Middle Ages, as do the first versions of it that we'd recognize today, containing honey, spices, and dried fruit. It was part of a larger trend of fruited breads showing up in Western Europe as dried fruit became more widely available. It was also expensive to make, so it was usually for special occasions like celebrating the harvest. Up to this point, fruitcake has no special connection to Christmas.

The next step in this evolution came in about the 17th century, when sugar became more affordable and widely available, and because of that, candying became a common way to preserve fruit. Soaking fruit in a sugar syrup not only sweetens it and gives it its telltale bright color, but it also makes it last pretty much forever, so candied fruits became a readily available option to add to fruitcakes. Around roughly the same time, it became common to load these cakes up with nuts as well.

Putting the "Sin" into "Sinfully Rich"

The result was something heavy and rich, and some even called it "sinfully rich"—and when they said that, they really meant it. So much so, that fruitcake was actually banned for much of the 18th century in continental Europe. And it wasn't doing much better in the newly formed United States. One anecdote, most likely apocryphal, tells of George Washington receiving a fruitcake as a gift, but refusing it on the grounds that, "It is unseemly for presidents to accept gifts weighing more than 80 pounds."

It wasn't until the next century that fruitcake really found its people, because the Victorians just loved the stuff. And not least of all because of their key contribution to its evolution, which was to preserve the cake by dousing it in alcohol. No proper British tea would be complete without a slice of fruitcake, and it became a popular wedding cake as well. Queen Victoria herself served fruitcake at her own wedding.

The rich treat became popular with many celebrations, including Christmas. As for how fruitcake became associated so strongly with Christmas, it's hard to identify a turning point. Just like sugarplums (see Chapter 1) and eggnog (see Chapter 4), fruitcake enjoyed a long history of being popular in its own right. Several tobacco companies even offered pipe and plug tobacco products labeled as "fruit cake" because the particular tobacco blends smelled and tasted like its namesake.

Because it was known as a wedding cake, a superstition formed that any unmarried person who placed a slice of wedding fruitcake under their pillow would dream of their future spouse.

But sometime between the 19th and 20th centuries, and especially here in America, it became more or less exclusively for Christmas. Making fruitcakes at Christmastime is central to the plot of Truman Capote's 1956 short story, "A Christmas Memory." Set during Prohibition, it tells of a young boy and his elderly cousin, who declares "it's fruitcake weather" in the opening scene. The pair set out to harvest wild pecans, and then to purchase ingredients—including bootleg

Meet the Fruitcake Lady

Marie Rudisill, one of the aunts who took in and raised Truman Capote for the part of the writer's life documented in "A Christmas Memory," forged her own literary career later in life, even becoming a Tonight Show *favorite as the wise and plain-spoken "Fruitcake Lady."*

Rudisill published her first book about Capote's childhood in 1983, when she was 72 years old. The 2000 publication of Fruitcake: Memories of Truman Capote and Sook *got her an invitation to* The Tonight Show *in December of that year, and on that visit she taught host Jay Leno and fellow guest Mel Gibson how to make fruitcakes.*

That segment led to subsequent appearances over the years, where she would show Leno the finer points of making other desserts and, eventually, answer viewers' questions in the "Ask the Fruitcake Lady" segment, which became so popular that she collected her advice in 2006's Ask the Fruitcake Lady: Everything You Would Already Know If You Had Any Sense.

The book hit shelves just weeks after her death at the age of 95. The week the book came out, The Tonight Show *remembered her with a highlight reel of her appearances on the show, including a kiss on the cheek she got from Tom Cruise.*

whiskey—from the "fruitcake fund" they scrape together throughout the year. The narrator describes the necessary ingredients: "cherries and citron, ginger and vanilla and canned Hawaiian pine-apple, rinds and raisins and walnuts and whiskey and oh, so much flour, butter, so many eggs, spices, flavorings: why, we'll need a pony to pull the buggy home." They make 30 fruitcakes in all, which they send to a ragtag assortment of "people who've struck our fancy," including President Roosevelt.

Not very long after the publication of Capote's story, it became very common—fashionable, even—to dislike fruitcake.

So . . . What Happened?

Given that fruitcake survived 1,400 or so years—making it through the Middle Ages, and becoming so popular that an entire continent thought that it should be banned for being *too* good, and receiving the endorsement of royalty—what happened? How did we turn the corner so quickly and so thoroughly, that fruitcake became the butt of so many jokes and the recipient of so much open hostility?

To put it simply: mass production. "Indeed, there are a lot of really bad fruitcakes out there," admits Isabelle Kirk, the blogger behind *Mondo Fruitcake*, a site dedicated to defending the honor of the much-maligned dessert.

And many of those bad fruitcakes arrived on the scene right around the time people started hating it—those commercially produced, mail-order monstrosities that came around in the early 20th century. Many people's first and last experience with fruitcake was a dry, flavorless doorstop of a cake that showed up in their mailbox.

Fruitcakes produced en masse, 1939. LIBRARY OF CONGRESS

Two Fruitcake Jokes That Shook the World

Like mothers-in-law and airplane food, fruitcakes have provided easy fodder for stand-up comics throughout the 20th century. But perhaps two televised jokes forever cemented the holiday dessert's reputation as being inedible and unwanted.

"Blame Johnny Carson," says Kirk. "He's the one who did that joke back in [1985] about there being just one fruitcake, and it gets passed around from person to person."

Pee-wee Herman took the cake calumny even further in the beloved 1988 TV special Christmas at Pee-wee's Playhouse. *A running joke throughout the show has Pee-wee giving all his pals very thoughtful and very specific gifts, and in return, he receives a fruitcake from each and every one of them. He's clearly disappointed until the end of the show—when he uses all the fruitcakes as bricks to build an extension onto the Playhouse.*

Many of us grew up with the jokes and the haters and the fruitcake tosses. Few adults who didn't have fruitcake as children would choose to try the boozy-tasting cake with the un-cake-like texture and studded with neon fruit. Maybe they're also turned off when learning how fruitcake is virtually indestructible, lasting for years or even centuries. In 2017 Arctic conservators reported finding a 106-year-old fruitcake, believed to have been brought there on a 1910 expedition of British explorer Robert Falcon Scott. In a statement, the conservators said the fruitcake was well preserved and looked and smelled edible.

So, we have at least one entire generation that grew up thinking we're just supposed to avoid fruitcake. According to one survey, 47% of people say if they received a fruitcake, they'd end up throwing it away. Another 11% said that they try to find someone to pawn it off on.

But for those dwindling number of fruitcake true believers, there's no such thing as a person who dislikes fruitcake, only a person who's never had a proper one. It sounds like what the world needs is not *less* fruitcake, but *better* fruitcake.

Green Cherries Are Optional: What Goes Into a Delicious Fruitcake?

Isabelle Kirk of Mondo Fruitcake *encourages the curious to break away from old notions about fruitcake—and those terrible mail-order horrors—because there's a new generation of bakers and cookbook writers exploring new ways to make the dessert more decadent and delicious.*

West Coast baker Robert Lambert has been making a name for himself, even among fruitcake haters, with his rich creations involving an array of nuts, fresh ginger, and candied fruit peel—not the obvious ones, but bergamot, Rangpur lime, blood orange, Buddha's hand citron, and the peel of the shekwasha, a rare Japanese aromatic. (Relax, traditionalists, he also includes glacée cherries and pineapple.)

Popular TV chef and cookbook author Nigella Lawson has the perfect solution for people put off by the big chunks of fruit and nut found in so many fruitcakes. Her Traditional Christmas Cake uses small fruits like currants and golden raisins (boiled in bourbon or brandy and then left to steep overnight) as well as featuring chopped nuts rather than whole ones. Those with an aversion or allergy to nuts might enjoy her Toffee Date Cake, in which the dates are incorporated into the batter rather than standing out discretely the way fruit often does within a fruitcake.

Dates, raisins, nuts, and brandy all make their way into Daryl Bruce's recipe, which the author swears is the fruitcake that even fruitcake-haters will love. (Bruce also notes, regarding why some people have a lifelong hatred of this holiday treat, "Store-bought fruitcake is not real fruitcake. It's simply a mix of a couple of raisins and nuts drowned in a vat of corn syrup loosely held together by some batter.")

CHAPTER 4

EGGNOG

The Creamy, Boozy, Eggy Beverage That Fueled a Riot

Christmassy beverages like hot chocolate and mulled cider are essential for toasting the season and sharing a cup of good cheer. The most Christmassy beverage of all just may be that sweet, golden, creamy concoction served with a sprinkling of nutmeg, and a cinnamon stick for stirring in the rum or brandy.

We've been drinking some version of eggnog since medieval times, even though it wasn't always called "eggnog." The eggnog we drink today may bear little to no resemblance to its forebears, but few things are as quintessentially Christmassy as the taste of eggnog.

Where did eggnog come from? How did taxes and trade help shape the modern drink? And what does the word "nog" mean, anyway?

Here are two things we know to be true:

1. As far back as the late 17th century in England, there was a strong beer known as "nog."
2. Going back hundreds of years earlier than that in England, certain alcoholic drinks were served in small carved wooden mugs called "noggins."

We don't know whether the word "eggnog" is in reference to 1 or 2. It may be neither because there's a third option: according to at least one historian, the word "eggnog" is a combination of "egg" and "grog." Grog was a slang term for the rum that was often added to the drink. So, there's some debate over the true origins of the term, and the drink has gone by other names like "milk punch" and "egg milk punch," which just doesn't have the same ring to it.

No matter where the term came from, most culinary historians will tell you that eggnog is based on a medieval British drink called posset, made from hot milk curdled with alcohol, either wine or ale, and flavored with spices. It was often used as a cold or flu remedy. Variations involved ingredients like fresh cream, eggs, and different spices. These were usually available only to the wealthy, and as such, it was often used when making toasts to prosperity.

For most of its life, posset wasn't associated exclusively with Christmas. It wasn't until it crossed the Atlantic and arrived in the colonies here in America that it not only became officially known as "eggnog." Its popularity was helped along by ramped up production among dairy farms. It was just starting to become a popular celebration drink closely associated with Christmastime.

"Spiked Eggnog"? Only If You Want to Live

These days, we refer to "spiked eggnog" as the kind with alcohol in it. But long ago, that was the *only* kind. "Spiked eggnog" is a retronym, a term created for an existing word to distinguish it from a more modern meaning. Just as there was no need to refer to an "acoustic guitar" in the days before electric guitars, so too was "spiked eggnog" simply known as eggnog for most of its existence. Back in the days before pasteurization and refrigeration, the addition of alcohol played an important part in making eggnog safe to drink. The libation never would have made it to the present day if the people who invented it had all gotten sick from food poisoning.

Make Mine Rum, If You Please

The addition of rum as the alcohol is another American contribution, and not necessarily because colonists preferred the taste of rum. During its time in England, it was usually spiked with ale or brandy. In the colonies, however, brandy was very heavily taxed while, thanks to a bustling trade with the Caribbean, rum was comparatively cheaper and more plentiful. Of course, you can spike it with almost anything.

Let's Make Eggnog Like George Washington

George Washington is known to have served an eggnog-like beverage to visitors at Mount Vernon. Legend has it that the recipe was Washington's own creation. The Old Farmer's Almanac has updated the recipe to include measurements suitable for a homemade batch.

"One quart cream, one quart milk, one dozen tablespoons sugar, one pint brandy, ½ pint rye whiskey, ½ pint Jamaica rum, ¼ pint sherry—mix liquor first, then separate yolks and whites of 12 eggs, add sugar to beaten yolks, mix well. Add milk and cream, slowly beating. Beat whites of eggs until stiff and fold slowly into mixture. Let set in cool place for several days. Taste frequently."

All Was Not Calm, All Was Not Bright

Whiskey is also commonly added to eggnog, or at least it was. And in 1826, a plan to add whiskey to eggnog went horribly awry. At West Point Academy, the cadets had been no strangers to drunken parties on and off campus. So, in 1826, superintendent General Thayer banned all alcohol on campus. Even getting drunk in one of the taverns across the Hudson River was grounds for expulsion.

When the cadets learned that the eggnog at the annual Christmas party would be alcohol-free, a group of them hatched a mischievous plan to remedy the situation: They took a boat across the Hudson to procure two gallons of whiskey and smuggle it back into the barracks.

On Christmas Eve, the cadets started pouring the spiked eggnog in one of their quarters. Word quickly spread, and the party grew larger and louder and drunker and rowdier. By four in the morning, the party had gotten noisy enough to wake up one of the faculty members, Captain Ethan Allen Hitchcock. Hitchcock attempted to break the party up, which only angered some of the cadets. They decided to harass Hitchcock by knocking on his bedroom door and running away.

Up until this point, the cadets were only having an illegal party. That alone was bad enough to warrant expulsion, but things quickly went from bad to worse. A patrolling officer was attacked while trying to restore order. Other cadets were breaking windows and damaging other property, and one cadet fired a shot into Hitchcock's room.

By six in the morning, the rowdiness was starting to die down. Several of the cadets who weren't involved in the drinking and rioting were helping to restore order. Many of the cadets showed up for formation barefoot, in torn uniforms, still drunk from the night before. It wasn't until after breakfast that morning that order was completely restored.

The story doesn't end there. In the days that followed, it was determined that of the 250 cadets enrolled at West Point at the time, 70 had taken part in the riot. Several were placed under house arrest and an official court inquiry began. The matter even made it to the desk of President John Quincy Adams, who actually got involved with the court-martial verdicts. Seventeen cadets were expelled or suspended.

The whole incident went down in history as the Eggnog Riot, sometimes also called the Grog Mutiny.

Tips from a Pro on Making Your Own Eggnog

Jeffrey Morgenthaler is the author of The Bar Book: Elements of Cocktail Technique *and was the bar manager at the famed Clyde Common in Portland, Oregon. Naturally, he has some suggestions on how to tackle this beloved but often complicated holiday concoction.*

"You just blend up a couple of eggs, a little bit of sugar. You don't use any ice—you just use the blender to mix it on low speed, add your alcohol and then your milk and your cream. And that's it.

"It really takes just a couple of minutes to make a batch of eggnog. Our eggnog at Clyde Common is añejo tequila, Amontillado sherry, with cream, milk, eggs, sugar, and nutmeg. So we do things slightly different. We like to have a little bit of fun with it. And I've always loved tequila and sherry together. Añejo tequila is, essentially, aged agave brandy, so that made a lot of sense to me. And the Amontillado sherry brings a nice kind of nuttiness to it. It's a really beautiful drink. We serve it in tea cups, you know, which is sort of a five- to six-ounce serving, because that's a really filling drink. You don't want to have too much of that. One or two, and I'm usually pretty good."

CHAPTER 5

CHRISTMAS DINNER

Tonight, We're Gonna Party Like It's 1899

Picture the scene: an ancient community somewhere in Northern Europe. For the people of this community, life revolves around the daily demands of agriculture: tending to fields and livestock, harvesting and stockpiling crops, making beer and wine. They awaken with the rising sun and grind out the chores of agricultural living for as long as daylight allows.

But not long after the annual harvest, that daylight grows shorter and the temperatures colder. Soon, there will be little work to be done in the fields because nothing is growing. And that means there won't be enough to feed the animals, so they slaughter all but a few for their meat and skins. As winter nears, the period of winemaking and beermaking are complete, and not a moment too soon.

And so, our ancient agricultural community finds itself with an abundance of food and drink, and plenty of time to enjoy it. They also have good reason to stay close together as winter closes in. It's a time for relaxing, indulging, and strengthening ties.

Thus, we have the beginnings of wintertime feasting and celebrating.

Long before these yearly feasts would have specific names and rituals, and long before they would have their own music, decorations, and special dishes, we had the simple reality of changing seasons and boom-and-bust food supplies.

We Like What We Like—Year after Year after Year

Fast forward to the present day where, like most of the traditions of Christmas, so too has the Christmas dinner become standardized across regions, generations, and even economic strata, to some extent. Yes, the Brits may still enjoy their Christmas pudding and mince pie, while Americans stick with their marshmallow–sweet potato casserole. Yes, there are still regional Christmas traditions here in America: Virginia with its traditional oysters, Louisiana with its gumbo. And yes, Christmas dinner can be extravagant or pedestrian. But gone are the ancient dishes of brawn and wild boar's head. Plum porridge (a beef stew thickened with breadcrumbs and dried fruit, once common at Christmas) has also vanished.

If you're planning a traditional Christmas meal in America, the overwhelming likelihood is that it will include mashed potatoes, cranberry relish, and roasted root vegetables. And at the center of it all, a stuffed turkey. It's a harvest-season meal of abundance and indulgence in the British tradition. It's also a meal that represents a snapshot in time, the final phase in an evolution that began centuries ago and, strangely, stopped evolving sometime in the 19th century. As Judith Flanders, historian and author of *Christmas: A Biography*, puts it: "In a holiday that is very fluid and evolving rapidly, the traditional Christmas dinner has not evolved. It's remained stuck in a 19th century time warp."

Carl Larsson's 1905 painting Christmas Eve *depicts a traditional Christmastime meal.* WIKIMEDIA COMMONS

According to the song, everybody knows a turkey and some mistletoe helps to make the season bright. But why? Our traditional Christmas dinner is, after all, just one of nearly infinite possibilities. The story of how we got to now has very much to do with economics, dropping infant mortality rates, a pig that's technically a fish, and overloaded stagecoaches.

It would take many centuries for wintertime feasting to merge with the observation of Christmas, and many centuries more for the concept to become widespread. Over the centuries a custom developed where the wealthy and powerful held grand banquets in December—sometimes, though not necessarily, on Christmas Day. As Judith Flanders tells it: "What you had was a long period when the greatest in the land would use Christmas Day as a day to entertain their dependents. That might be the people who work for them and their political allies. These meals weren't Christmas meals as we know them. They were simply grand banquets. They would have mutton, beef, and venison. From the sixteenth century in Europe, you might have turkeys."

Goose Clubs

Even though goose was more affordable than beef, that doesn't mean it was within easy reach for most families. Many working-class households would save all year for such a luxury, and belonging to a "goose club" was a common way to ensure that there would be a roast goose on the table for Christmas dinner.

Goose clubs were typically organized by the landlord of the local pub, who often bred geese in the land behind the pub. Each week, participants would contribute a small amount (typically a ha'penny) to a sort of savings account. By year's end, participants received their goose. Sometimes, goose clubs would also involve a lottery where the winner received the fattest goose.

Those grand banquets, and the scenes described by Tusser, certainly didn't adhere to the church's rules around restraint and penance, nor its general warnings against overindulgence. They were more secular affairs that flouted church guidance. But the church did influence Christmas dinner for a time, albeit probably unintentionally. Brawn (to use the modern spelling) is a cold cut made of pork or wild boar pressed into a mold. Americans nowadays know this as "head cheese." It's unclear exactly how, but the church classified brawn as fish, not meat, and so it became heavily associated with Christmas.

Thankfully, brawn eventually lost its vaunted status at the Christmas dinner table, but the beef, mutton, and venison remained staples at the tables of the wealthy. As we see our familiar Christmas dinner start to take shape in England during the 18th and 19th centuries, we see the effects of the wealth divide. For the rich, roast beef was the high point of luxury. (Though there are some known examples of the rich serving swan and peacock.) For those who couldn't afford it, goose was the go-to for many years.

This poem from English poet Thomas Tusser, published sometime between 1557 and 1577, includes an early description of an ideal Christmas feast:

CHRISTMAS HUSBANDLIE FARE

1. Good husband and huswife now cheefly be glad,
   things handsom to haue, as they ought to be had;
   They both doo prouide against Christmas doo come,
   to welcome good neighbour, good cheere to haue some.

2. Good bread and good drinke, a good fier in the hall,
   brawne, pudding and souse, and good mustard withall.

3. Beefe, mutton, and porke, shred pies of the best,
   pig, veale, goose and capon, and turkey well drest;
   Cheese, apples and nuts, ioly Carols to heare,
   as then in the countrie is counted good cheare.

4. What cost to good husband is any of this?
   good houshold prouision onely it is.
   Of other the like, I doo leaue out a menie,
   that costeth the husbandman neuer a penie.

Gobble Gobble

The version of the British Christmas dinner we know today is firmly fixed as a prosperous upper-middle-class Victorian family celebration meal. And the finishing touch made by the Victorians was the wide adoption of the turkey as the main Christmas bird. The turkey, native to North America, was brought to Europe in the 16th century, and King Henry VIII is thought to be the first monarch to have turkey for Christmas.

The transition was complete by the time Charles Dickens wrote *A Christmas Carol*, which includes the iconic scene just after Scrooge has his epiphany:

> "Here's the Turkey. Hallo! Whoop! How are you! Merry Christmas!"
>
> It was a Turkey! He never could have stood upon his legs, that bird. He would have snapped 'em short off in a minute, like sticks of sealing-wax.
>
> "Why, it's impossible to carry that to Camden Town," said Scrooge. "You must have a cab."

The embrace of turkeys was unlikely for a number of reasons. In the first place, in the days before refrigeration, farmers would walk their animals to market to be slaughtered on the spot. Turkeys don't travel well, due to their delicate feet. Not only that, but they tended to lose considerable weight on the way to market and had to be fattened up at the market before they were viable for sale. For these reasons, they were expensive. But they were large, much larger than a goose, and that helps to explain their popularity.

Perhaps one of the more surprising reasons they became so popular was the size of late-18th and early-19th-century families. Infant mortality during the Victorian era was still very high. In some parts of London, the death rate for children under five years of age was as high as 33%. But overall, those numbers were trending downward, and that meant that larger families were becoming more common. The size of the turkey, as compared to a goose, made it the obvious choice for families that could afford it.

Turkeys also became part of a long-standing tradition of the 18th and 19th centuries involving gift-giving in Britain. People living in the country would send their city friends some sort of bird for Christmas. And the reliable way to send something before there were railroads was on a stagecoach. Sending turkeys by stagecoach had become so in-demand that it was not uncommon to refuse human passengers to save room for the turkeys.

Freedom from Want

Norman Rockwell's Freedom from Want *depicts a typical holiday meal.*
US NATIONAL ARCHIVES AND RECORDS ADMINISTRATION

It's ironic that a bird native to North America had to travel to England before it could become the centerpiece of the American Christmas dinner. The British Christmas dinner crossed the Atlantic to an America where Christmas was largely ignored, or confined to small, regionally inspired celebrations. The post–Civil War period was a time of quickly rising industrialization in America, and a blending of cultural influences among a massive wave of immigration from Europe. Both of these factors would

Inventing a Christmas Meal

While the Christmas meal has been shaped by history and tradition, in some places, it has been shaped more by popular culture and advertising. In Japan, for example, Christmas wasn't a common seasonal event until the 1960s. Local bakers and confectioners began offering special seasonal treats for people to serve at Christmas parties. The "traditional" Japanese Christmas cake (a sponge cake topped with whipped cream and strawberries) was born.

KFC (then known as Kentucky Fried Chicken) came to Japan in the early 1970s. A member of the sales team overheard a foreign customer say during the Christmas season, "I can't get turkey in Japan, so I have no choice but to celebrate Christmas with Kentucky Fried Chicken." Sensing an opportunity, the company created a marketing campaign in 1974 to promote KFC as a Christmas meal. Decades later, the campaign is still a hit, with KFCs taking orders weeks in advance, and Christmas Eve being the busiest day of the year.

help give rise to the American Christmas. Why, then, did the British dinner win the day? Why not the Swedish version, which favored cod? Or the German version, with its goose or carp?

Before, and well after, America declared independence, England's imperial influence was strong, especially among the cultural elite. Colonial Americans had adopted the turkey as a celebration food, a tradition that held firm, and became a symbol of assimilation into American culture for immigrants.

Helping to solidify all of this was a rapidly growing print media, which allowed for specific descriptions of Christmas fare to become wide-reaching and quickly socialized. One such example is a short story titled "His Christmas Turkey," published in a Kansas newspaper in 1891, which depicts a comic mishap involving a turkey hunt for Christmas dinner.

Turkey hunts would eventually give way to advances in farming, breeding, refrigeration, and distribution. By the middle of the 20th century, Norman Rockwell's "Freedom from Want" painting became the iconic image of the American holiday meal.

Christmas dinner as we know it today remains stuck in the late 19th century as a reflection of upper-middle-class tastes, and foods that were seasonally and locally available in Britain. Nowadays, with a global food supply, season and location no longer factor into what we can eat, and when. Perhaps ironically, we're in the midst of a growing trend to eat more seasonally, locally, and sustainably. Christmas dinner as we know it will very likely remain unchanged from its 19th century time warp for generations to come.

CHAPTER 6

WASSAIL

Drunken Trick-or-Treating—for the Good of Society!

Some words are both nouns and verbs depending on the context. For example, you can milk a cow, or you can drink some milk. You can exit a room by using the exit or dust your furniture to remove the dust. Now, if you're a fan of grammar (and really, who isn't?) you'll know that a verb that's derived from a noun is called a denominal verb, and the opposite—a noun derived from a verb—is called a deverbal noun.

But what do you call a word that's both a thing you say and a thing you do? A thing you make, a state of mind, an event, a concoction, an expression of good health, and sometimes a reference to raucous partying? Well, when it comes to Christmas traditions, you call it wassail.

Nowadays, wassail—like sugarplums (see Chapter 1) or hot buttered rum—is a part of the Christmas season that most of us experience mainly through references in songs, stories, and artwork. But this old English custom is about much more

Did You Know?

According to historian Gerry Bowler, in the West Country, it was customary to wassail oxen on Twelfth Night (the finale of the traditional Christmas season). People took the wassail bowl into the stalls and placed a cake on the ox's horns.

than sharing a cup of good cheer: It's about one of the parts of Christmas that's most likely destined to remain stuck in Christmas past, the notion of inverting the normal rules of social order, and all with a little help from alcohol.

Down Is Up, Wrong Is Right—And I'll Drink to That

A term you don't hear a lot anymore, and certainly not when it comes to Christmas, is "social inversion." As the name suggests, it has to do with role reversals and turning social rules and norms inside out. It was once a common theme in the ancient Roman celebration of Saturnalia. And social inversion was also once a major part of the Christmas celebration. Some churches elected a child to be a "boy bishop" who presided over the ceremony. Other cultures adopted a Lord of Misrule, a jester-like figure who led the festivities. So, what does any of this have to do with wassail?

A servant places a silver wassail bowl. From "Old Christmas" in The Sketch Book of Washington Irving *(1886).*
PROJECT GUTENBERG

"What happens with wassail is it is fundamentally a rite of crossing the threshold," says Conrad Bladey, the author of *The Book of Wassail*, a five-volume look into wassail literature, music, folklore, and recipes. "The people who are poor workers on the estate could go to the wealthy person's house and perform—not as beggars, but as good people with self-esteem. The master of the house would let them in and feed them and treat them very well, so that he would be on their good side. And they might return again next year. They could express their problems and needs to him at the time, and he could help provide for them, because he depended upon them for his livelihood."

The word "wassail" is from the Old English "ves heill," literally, "Be thou hale" or, in other words, "To your health." It was a toast, like "Cheers!" or the Irish "Sláinte!" But the significance was not necessarily the wish for good health, but the dynamic of who was wishing it for whom.

"At the end of *A Christmas Carol*, Scrooge meets with Cratchit," notes Bladey, "and they have a glass of Smoking Bishop, and therefore they link up together and become more friendly, at least for a while."

Smoking Bishop is a kind of mulled punch commonly served at banquets in a bowl resembling a bishop's mitre, and most people think of wassail as something along these lines. But the truth is, wassail can be almost anything, and in fact it has been many things throughout time.

According to Bladey, "In the apple-growing countries and cider countries, it's cider with ale in it, and the spices are the Christmas spices: allspice, ginger, cinnamon. It's served hot—but not too hot, because if it's too hot, the alcohol will go away. Then in the 18th century, we have a great blossoming of possets and egg-based beverages: eggnogs, all sorts of things made with eggs and filled with spices and sugar. That was a very legitimate wassail. But these days, we've got wassail shooters made of Jell-O and wassail."

"Christmas
for
Ever!"

A Cornucopia You Can Drink

One traditional version originates from the summertime celebration of Lammas, honoring the first fruits of the harvest. "That dates way back to the 17th century," says Bladey, "and that was wassail with baked apples in it. When you take it out of the broiler, the apple—with a darkened skin, almost black—explodes and shoots these fibers out through the fluid. It sort of looks like angel-hair pasta. It makes a very tasty drink; sometimes they actually made almost a pudding."

The Most Important Thing about Wassail

Notes Bladey, "The most important thing about wassail is that it's an essential human device, which is important for bringing people together socially who do not agree with each other. It's very important to break down the boundaries of people, cross over the threshold, and look out for one another. But it's not something that's naturally human—it has to be contrived."

So we have a tradition of drinking to one's health in a socially atypical setting, and we have a drink that's generally regionally inspired, but for the most part tends to be some kind of spiked punch with winter spices.

There are other variations on the wassail tradition: Devonshire farmers would chant and drink in their orchards to encourage a strong crop. In other parts, farmers would place bread or cake on the horns of an ox. There's even mention of wassailing beehives. But how did wassail become not just a toast or a drink, but an activity as in, "Here we come a-wassailing"? And what does that even mean?

Like Trick-or-Treating. But with Booze.

"That's evolved into different customs and different versions," notes Bladey. "At first, ordinary people would travel around in groups, and instead of begging, they would sing a song, and in return for the song, they would cross the threshold to the master's house."

So rather than the wealthy inviting the poor into their homes, the poor started going from home to home, almost like trick-or-treating or caroling. But with booze.

Bladey continues, "The next thing that happened is that these people became professional craftsmen. Every year, the same group of guys get together, get the kit together, dress up, and they go from door to door. It became formalized. And it's still done in England, in a formal way—people go door to door, and they'll perform a mummers play."

The "Gloucester Wassail" Song

As wassail expert Conrad Bladey points out, there are all kinds of contemporary wassail recipes, from the meticulous to the easy. (Several online recipes include ingredients like Tang and Country Time powdered drink mixes.)

But whatever your concoction, you can stay true to the beverage's history by singing along to the traditional "Gloucester Wassail" Christmas carol, which is also known as "The Wassail Bowl" or "Wassail! Wassail! All Over the Town."

CHORUS (to be sung between every verse):
Wassail! wassail! all over the town,
Our toast it is white and our ale it is brown;
Our bowl it is made of the white maple tree;
With the wassailing bowl, we'll drink to thee.

Here's to our horse, and to his right ear,
God send our master a happy new year:
A happy new year as e'er he did see,
With my wassailing bowl I drink to thee.

So here is to Cherry and to his right cheek
Pray God send our master a good piece of beef
And a good piece of beef that may we all see
With the wassailing bowl, we'll drink to thee.

Here's to our mare, and to her right eye,
God send our mistress a good Christmas pie;
A good Christmas pie as e'er I did see,
With my wassailing bowl I drink to thee.

So here is to Broad Mary and to her broad horn
May God send our master a good crop of corn
And a good crop of corn that may we all see
With the wassailing bowl, we'll drink to thee.

And here is to Fillpail and to her left ear
Pray God send our master a happy New Year
And a happy New Year as e'er he did see
With the wassailing bowl, we'll drink to thee.

Here's to our cow, and to her long tail,
God send our master us never may fail
Of a cup of good beer: I pray you draw near,
And our jolly wassail it's then you shall hear.

Come butler, come fill us a bowl of the best
Then we hope that your soul in heaven may rest
But if you do draw us a bowl of the small
Then down shall go butler, bowl and all.

Be here any maids? I suppose here be some;
Sure they will not let young men stand on the cold stone!
Sing hey O, maids! come trole back the pin,
And the fairest maid in the house let us all in.

Then here's to the maid in the lily white smock
Who tripped to the door and slipped back the lock
Who tripped to the door and pulled back the pin
For to let these jolly wassailers in.

And later it became a different kind of activity: a party. "At the end of the 19th century," observes Bladey, "you have what I call the wassail masque or the Christmas masque, which is not the court masque. It's an evolution of that into a large hall, which could be a court hall or the King's hall or a landowner's hall—a big hall where people got together and feasted. And they took apart all of the customs and dropped them all into the same sort of play. So you have the Yule log, wassailing, people dressed up, and they had processions, where people drank and ate."

And since "wassail" has had many meanings over time, so too has it had different connotations. What started as a simple toast to good health eventually took a turn. "In the 19th century, in novels," says Bladey, "it becomes something terrible. Prior to that, in literature, wassailing was holy and sacred."

Today, and especially in America, wassail has largely fallen by the wayside. Again, we experience it mostly by way of its mentions in Christmas music and literature, or maybe by trying a recipe that you find on the internet. But this Christmas season, you might try bringing a little more wassail into your celebration, now that you know it's about much more than a specific toast or drink.

CHAPTER 7

GINGERBREAD

The House That Grimm (Probably) Built

Remember Hansel and Gretel? If you wanted to create something specifically designed to tempt a child beyond all hope of self-control, you would create a gingerbread house. Families everywhere construct these cookie creations every Christmas, adorning them with gumdrops, candy canes, chocolate buttons, and lots and lots of icing. And however skillful or stale the results, children everywhere can't wait to devour them.

But how, exactly, did this tradition start? It's a bit of a mystery. One thing's certain: before there could be gingerbread houses or gingerbread men, first there needed to be gingerbread. And for that, of course, there needed to be ginger.

Let's go back all the way to the turn of the 11th century. Traders returning from the Middle East were just starting to introduce the ginger root to Western Europe. At first it was used medicinally, to treat digestive issues and even hangovers. Later, it was used as a spice.

It was also discovered that ginger could be a good preservative. This is probably a big part of the reason it caught on: Preserving food was really important in those days before packaging and refrigeration.

First Lady Rosalynn Carter, looking at a gingerbread house with White House Pastry Chef Roland Mesnier, at the White House, 1979. LIBRARY OF CONGRESS

Spoiler Alert: Gingerbread Isn't Actually Bread at All

It's difficult to pinpoint the first examples of gingerbread, or what it may have been like. Recipes certainly would have varied from region to region. By the 13th century, one form of gingerbread was popular in Poland.

The word itself has a surprising history, because maybe you've noticed that most gingerbread—whether soft, or the crisp, cookie-like kind, or the moist, dense cake-like kind—isn't really like bread at all. That's because the word is actually a misnomer. The original term was "gingembrat," from the Old French term meaning simply "preserved ginger." The word mutated over time, and by the 1500s, a more recognizable form emerged in English, with spellings like gingbreade, gynbred, gingbread.

If you're used to your gingerbread sweetly spiced with cinnamon, nutmeg, and molasses, you probably wouldn't like some of the earlier forms of gingerbread, which often called for licorice, pepper, and ale. Typically made with breadcrumbs for structure, the result was more like a confection than a cake or a bread.

Let's Make Gingerbread Like It's 1673

Looking for an authentically ancient gingerbread recipe? Try this one from the 1673 cookbook, Lady Barbara Fleming's Manuscript Receipt Book. *But don't expect it to taste anything like the gingerbread you're used to. Oh, and those aren't typos below; they're the original 17th-century English spellings!*

Take a quart of honey, put it into a great skillet on the fire and when it begineth to seeth, put thereto a pint of strong ale, & scum it clear, then put soo much grated bread as will make it like unto dow and put thereto halfe a pound of Liquorish, as much Aniseeds, and a quarter of a pound of ginger being finely searced with two ounces of graines, then take it out of your skillet and worke it on a table as you doo flower to dough to make it stiffe, then make it in cakes, put powder of Liquorish and Aniseeds upon your moulds so it cleave not and so lay them upon a board till they be dry, then lay them up in boxes.

Gradually, flour replaced breadcrumbs, and different regions left their own distinctive mark on gingerbread. Its color could be light or dark, its flavor sweet or spicy, its texture soft or crisp.

Gingerbread: The Funnel Cake of an Earlier Era

Like many Christmas foods, gingerbread didn't start out with an exclusive connection to the holiday. For centuries in Europe, it was a popular food served at fairs and festivals, some of which came to be known as Gingerbread Fairs. The gingerbread sold at these festivals was often stamped with ornate, hand-carved molds to create images of saints and other important religious characters. It would be dusted with sugar to highlight the impression from the mold, or often gilded and iced. The creation of religious icons was seen as a sacred and prestigious practice, so European royalty allowed gingerbread to be prepared only by specially trained gingerbread guild members (except during Christmas and Easter). And artisan guilds of mold makers would work exclusively with gingerbread makers. Gingerbread molds are true works of art, and many are on display in museums in Europe.

Nuremberg in Germany was the junction for several trade routes, and had access to spices not available elsewhere. As a result, Nuremberg attracted the best bakers and became famous for its gingerbread cakes and cookies, which included cardamom, cloves, cinnamon, pepper, anise, and ginger. Perhaps the beginnings of a special connection to Christmas was in Nuremberg, where gingerbread was a particularly popular item sold at the famous Christkindlesmarkt (and remains so to this day).

Of course, molded gingerbread pieces eventually gave way to the now familiar gingerbread man. The first documented example of gingerbread cut into a figure-shaped cookie was in the 16th century, when Queen Elizabeth I had the gingerbread figures made and presented in the likeness of some of her important guests.

"AND I CAN RUN AWAY FROM YOU. I CAN!"

In 1875, St. Nicholas Magazine (a popular monthly children's magazine) published "The Gingerbread Boy." The story tells of a gingerbread cookie that jumps out of the oven and runs away. As he runs, a growing group of characters pursue him, but he manages to evade them all, taunting them as he goes. In the final lines of the story, a fox joins the hunt, who the Gingerbread Boy taunts, saying:

> I've run away from a little old woman,
> A little old man,
> A barn full of thresh-ers,
> A field full of mow-ers,
> A cow and a pig,
> And I can run a-way from you. I can!

The fox, however, catches and eats the Gingerbread Boy in the end.

"The Gingerbread Boy" was the first print publication of the story, based on a folktale. Folktales involving runaway food were once common in many parts of the world. Other examples include Germany's "The Runaway Pancake," Ireland's "The Wonderful Cake," and Russia's "The Devil in the Dough-Pan."

The story has been retold and republished many times, with some versions bearing the title "The Gingerbread Man," and including the famous line:

> Run, run as fast as you can!
> You cannot catch me. I am the Gingerbread Man!

It should come as no surprise that we would eventually make houses out of gingerbread, when you consider that it has a long history of being turned into other eye-catching works of art. But here's where things get interesting: We know that gingerbread houses showed up in Germany sometime in the 19th century, but why is a bit of a mystery.

It's Both Residential and Edible

There's no doubt they became popular because of the Brothers Grimm. When they collected volumes of German fairy tales, they found one about Hansel and Gretel, which the brothers published in 1812. In the story, two children discover a house in the woods made of cake and candies, created by a witch. In fact, in Germany, gingerbread houses are still referred to as "Hexenhausel" or "witches houses."

But it's not entirely certain whether actual gingerbread houses were already a common thing before that. What is certain is that after that 1812 publication, bakers in Germany started selling ornamented, fairy-tale-style gingerbread houses, which became popular during Christmas. That tradition came to America with the German immigrants who settled in Pennsylvania.

The gingerbread house that tempted Hansel and Gretel.
NEW YORK PUBLIC LIBRARY DIGITAL COLLECTIONS

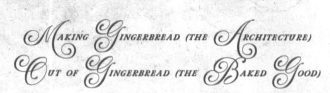

Making Gingerbread (the Architecture) Out of Gingerbread (the Baked Good)

It's interesting that the word "gingerbread" is also used to describe the intricate fretwork you see in some styles of architecture, like you see in those Victorian "Painted Ladies" in San Francisco. So, it was only a matter of time before someone would build an actual San Francisco Victorian out of gingerbread.

"The holiday display at the Fairmont San Francisco is really a destination," says Melissa Ferrar, director of marketing communications for San Francisco's Fairmont Hotel. "It's become this tradition for people to come and visit the hotel [at the holidays]."

Every year, the Fairmont creates a life-sized gingerbread house—you can actually walk inside it—and puts it on display in the lobby. "It's an experience you can participate in," says Ferrar. "It's seeing kids see this giant gingerbread house, and their eyes lighting up, but also seeing the adults—it kind of brings out the kid in the adults. So it's just an amazing and fun experience for everyone involved."

Thousands of people come to see it each year, and this thing includes almost 8,000 individual gingerbread bricks, 700 pounds of candy, and a ton of royal icing. Don't worry, it's San Francisco, so everything's composted afterward. Everything, that is, that doesn't fall into the sneaky little hands of hungry visitors.

"It's like Willy Wonka, you know, it's there right in front of them," notes Ferrar. "And I think people just can't help themselves sometimes. But we do have signs saying 'Santa Is Watching.'"

Gingerbread Crosses the Atlantic

Gingerbread came to the Americas with settlers from Europe. Amelia Simmons's 1796 book, *American Cookery* (known as the first American cookbook) contained several recipes for gingerbread, including one attributed to George Washington's mother. *American Cookery* was a very influential book, which helped spread gingerbread across America.

Gingerbread House Tips from the Pros

Are your gingerbread houses ramshackle? Do they have a tendency to fall apart like a special effect in Earthquake? Do you start out making a mansion and wind up with a hovel? These construction tips might come in handy:

- This is not the place for chewy gingerbread. Susan Reid from King Arthur Flour (and the former Food Editor of Sift magazine) advises that you go heavy with the flour when making your batter. "If you were going to make a cookie out of it, it'd be a pretty dry cookie. The more moisture you have in gingerbread, the flimsier—and you don't want flexible walls. You're trying to make something that's going to be rigid." Reid also recommends chilling your batter before you roll it out, to give the flour more opportunity to absorb any moisture.

- Decorate, then assemble. It's tempting to start with putting the walls and roof in place and then adding the candy décor, but you'll find the pieces are easier to decorate if they're flat on the table and not already standing at a 90-degree angle.

- Your icing should resemble meringue. Remember, this icing isn't just decorative—it's architectural. Experts recommend creating icing that contains egg whites and cream of tartar to really bulk your glaze up to pastry-cement levels. Reid notes that egg whites in icing are safe to eat, because the lack of water makes it impossible for bacteria to form.

- Big candy makes a big impression. If you've got the piping-bag skills to delicately decorate your gingerbread house with intricate designs, then go for it. For the rest of us—vividly striped candy sticks or oversized lollipops will cover up big stretches of plain brown exterior.

- For stained-glass windows, Reid prefers Jolly Rancher hard candies. "I put the individual colors in a sandwich bag," she suggests, "and I bash them up a bit with my rolling pin. Then I put the crushed-up candies on a baking sheet and let them melt together. They'll melt faster if they're crushed first."

- Search online for blueprints. Unless you've got cookie cutters the right size and shape to create your pieces, several websites offer templates that will take the guesswork out of measuring and shaping.

CHAPTER 8

CANDY CANES

A Sweet Mystery

Many of our most treasured and familiar Christmas traditions are packed with symbolic meaning. The circular shape of a wreath, and the holly and ivy it's made from, are all said to represent eternal life. By some accounts, the ingredients in a mince pie represent the gifts of the Magi. And a Christmas candle is often said to represent the Star of Bethlehem.

One of the most ubiquitous sights and flavors of the season is a symphony of symbolism in its own right. Its white color represents purity and rejection of sin; its peppermint flavor is a reference to hyssop, a mint-like herb that appears several times in the Old Testament for ceremonial cleansing of houses, among other things. The red stripes represent blood. And of course, the shape, roughly the length and diameter of a pencil, is bent at the bottom into a crook to form a letter "J" for "Jesus." Maybe you've even heard that these items were used as a way for Christians to secretly identify one another during times of persecution.

Except . . . *none of that is actually true.* Just as with the claim that the gifts from "The Twelve Days of Christmas" (see Chapter 22) are secretly metaphors for biblical stories, so too has the humble candy cane been given a second life in the realm of myth, retrofitted and superimposed upon something with a completely different origin story. There is no record at all to suggest the candy canes were created with any of this symbolism in mind. (If they were wouldn't they be called candy Js? And wouldn't the red symbolizing blood be a more appropriate symbol for Easter than Christmas?)

Besides, it's pretty well established already that candy canes were actually created way back in 1670 in Cologne, Germany, as a way of inducing children to behave in church. The choir master of the Cologne Cathedral needed to keep children quiet during ceremonies involving the church's live nativity scene, so he went to a local confectioner, and asked him to create some white peppermint sticks, which were already common at the time, but to bend the top to form the shape of a shepherd's cane. If the kids were busy with their candy canes, they wouldn't talk so much.

Except . . . none of *that* is actually well established either. Well circulated, yes; widely accepted, sure. But the idea that candy canes a) came from Germany, b) were the idea of a choir master, c) were given out in church, and d) were meant to symbolize a shepherd's cane, is about as historically supported as that first theory. There is simply nothing in the way of documentation or artifact to support this story.

So, What's the Real Story, Then?

For something so closely tied to Christmas, at least these days, and whose very image and flavor is practically synonymous with the season, and for a season whose many traditions contain centuries or millennia's worth of history and culture, it may be surprising to realize that candy canes are something of a sweet mystery.

Here's what we do know: Candy sticks have been around for centuries; they were usually plain white and often flavored with peppermint, among other flavors. Then, as now, run-of-the-mill candy sticks were enjoyed all throughout the year. Somewhere along the way, confectioners figured out how to add decorative stripes to candy. And somewhere else along the way, someone thought to bend a candy stick into the shape of a cane.

And here's something else we know—the first recorded English-language references to candy canes come not from 1670 or anywhere close to the time they were supposedly created, but nearly two centuries later. The first known reference was in 1866, in the story "Tom Luther's Stockings," published in *Ballou's Monthly Magazine*, which features a casual mention of candy canes in a candy shop window, but no description of them beyond that.

The first recorded reference to candy canes being specifically connected with Christmas didn't appear until almost a decade later. That came in another magazine, one for young readers called *The Nursery*. In 1874, a story titled "Benny's Letter" included a child's letter to Santa Claus asking for, among other things, a candy cane. His wish list also included things that are common at Christmas but not exclusive to it, like almonds and a pencil.

So, we can deduce that somewhere between the late 19th century and early 20th, candy canes became not only associated with Christmas, but also pretty much exclusively so. Other popular Christmas items have followed a similar course. Fruitcake (see Chapter 3), for example, was once a common cake for all celebrations, like weddings. Eggnog (see Chapter 4) used to be a common alcoholic beverage enjoyed year-round. That makes candy canes one of a very small number of candies enjoyed only at a certain time of year.

Novelty Candy-Cane Flavors That Might Actually Ruin Christmas

In the 21st century, candy canes have broken out of their peppermint paradigm to branch out in exciting new directions. If you like the taste of confectionary favorites like Sour Patch Kids, Starburst, Red Hots, and SweetTarts—or sodas like Orange Crush and A&W Root Beer—there's a candy cane out there to match those popular flavors.

But then there are the novelty candy canes, the ones that exist solely as a gag gift, or perhaps for some food blogger to eat as a dare. If these striped nightmares (which, for many, add a whole other meaning to "gag gift") are your cup of cocoa, more power to you, but don't go putting them in anyone else's stocking unless you ask permission first:

- *Gravy: A staple of Christmas dinner, great with meat and potatoes, but gravy was just never meant to align itself with hard candy.*
- *Rotisserie Chicken: Just . . . no.*
- *Coal: While this flavor is clearly meant to bring to mind Santa's punishment for naughty children, there actually was a recent food trend of people putting coal into ice cream and other foods, ostensibly for health reasons. Still, forget it.*
- *Pizza: If you're really craving the flavor of pizza, an actual pizza is just a phone call or a few keyboard clicks away. Absolutely not.*
- *Wasabi: As far as we know, no one has tried to foist a sushi-flavored candy cane onto the market, but this spicy condiment is the next-worst idea.*
- *Kale: Here's the thing—no one eats kale for the flavor. You either want the fiber, or the crunch, or the dietary value.*
- *Bacon / Mac and Cheese: Sure, the real things are great, but an artificial flavor attached to a Christmas treat? Pass.*
- *Clamdy Canes: That's correct, candy canes that taste like clams. No. No. No. No. No.*

It's a Confection, and It's a Decoration

And possibly one more reason they're so closely linked to Christmas, at least here in America, is because their hook shape makes them perfect for hanging on a Christmas tree. In fact, in 1882, eight years after the publication of "Benny's Letter," another short story, this one published in *Babyland* magazine, mentions hanging the candy on the branches of a Christmas tree. Some have even gone as far as speculating—and it is just speculation—that that is the true origin of the hooked-cane shape, because it was once common to decorate Christmas trees with all kinds of food items, like cookies and fruit. Some have theorized that the idea of the cane was specifically to accommodate hanging them on the tree.

"It's one of the few candies and perhaps the only candy that's really used as much as a decoration, as [it] is a piece of candy to eat." So says Kirk Vashaw, the CEO of Spangler Candy in Ohio. They're the largest producer of candy canes in America, and they produce about half of all the world's candy canes. If you've ever had a candy cane, it was almost certainly made by Spangler.

"The United States has a tradition of people decorating their Christmas trees with candy canes, which is not a tradition in most other countries," notes Vashaw. "But in the United States, that's where most of the candy-cane volume is in the world, and it is because of that tradition of decorating the Christmas trees."

But even though candy canes are a seasonal treat for you and me, they're daily work for Spangler. For Vashaw, "it's Christmas every day. We make candy canes throughout the year."

So just what kind of production schedule is necessary to keep the shelves stocked and the Christmas trees decorated and the office candy bowls full? "We make about 2.7 million candy canes every day, and we usually start making for the following Christmas," Vashaw reveals. "We might start around November 1 for the following year."

And even though much of the work is done by machines—the first patent for a candy-cane machine is about a hundred years old—there's still some old-world confectionery craftsmanship in every candy cane you eat.

According to Vashaw, "The striping process is very manual, and it's one of the hardest jobs that we have in our factory, in the sense that it takes a while to get good at it. Striping a candy cane is still done by hand, so in some sense, they're all handmade."

In a given year Spangler makes about 650 million candy canes, serving a $100 million retail market. And given everything we've learned so far, we can say that red-striped and mint-flavored candy canes are the traditional form. But we don't know exactly what we're talking about. When we say "traditional," it's pretty likely that traditional candy canes were invented or at least finalized sometime in the 19th century. And they stayed that way until about 20 years ago.

"In the last 20 years, there's been more we call flavored candy canes," says Vashaw. "For example, we make a Jelly Belly Candy Cane that has Jelly Belly flavors in it, and Jelly Belly colors, and there are Starburst candy canes, and there are chocolate mint candy canes, and those flavored candy canes typically are eaten at a higher percentage. A lot of them don't actually make it to the tree—they get eaten ahead of time."

And you've seen some of those odd ones on the shelves or shared on social media. (See side-bar.) Kale flavored candy canes, mac-and-cheese flavored, dill-pickle flavored. (That last one actually sounds pretty good.) Even though we don't know the true origins of the candy cane, we do know that we're not yet done experimenting with this iconic Christmas treat.

Did You Know?

Bunte Brothers, a Chicago candy company founded in 1876, filed one of the earliest patents for candy-cane-making machines in the early 1920s.

PART II

Santa Claus, Rudolph the Red-Nosed Reindeer, even Charlie Brown. They're the characters behind the stories and legends that bring magic to our childhood Christmas and nostalgia ever after. They're the stuff of not only the stories they populate, but also the stories of their creation. How did an historical bishop from what is now Turkey go on to become Santa Claus? Why are all the classic Christmas cartoons from the 1960s? Is the story of Rudolph a semi-autobiography? Let's find out.

CHAPTER 9

SANTA CLAUS

From Bishop's Robes to a Flying Sleigh

Imagine a large roomful of people. It's a good mix of male and female, young and old, from all over the world and all walks of life. You're in this imaginary room, too, and you're there to run a little experiment.

You hand each person a sheet of paper and a set of crayons and ask them to perform one simple task: draw a picture of Santa Claus. When everyone is finished, how much variation do you think you'd see? Not variation in artistic ability, but variation in ideas about what Santa Claus looks like. Probably not very much at all.

Almost certainly, every picture depicts an old man with a white beard. He's likely wearing a red fur suit with white trim, and a matching hat with a pom-pom on its pointed tip. In other words, the image of Santa is universal and standardized. The only things that change are the small details, like whether he wears gloves or mittens. It wasn't always this way.

Santa Claus is among the most recognizable figures in the world. But even though he's been around for centuries, the image of him that we all recognize today, of a grandfatherly gift giver riding a magic sleigh, is surprisingly new.

Exactly how did Saint Nicholas become Santa Claus? Or should we say Kris Kringle? And why does he have so many names, anyway? That's a story 1,700 years in the making, and one that isn't

"Merry Old Santa Claus," Thomas Nast's most famous illustration of Santa Claus, published in Harper's Weekly *(1881).* GETTY IMAGES

finished yet. It's a blurry mixture of fact and legend—a tale of miracles and murder, of torture and tomb raiders, of the rise of print media and advertising, and much more.

Before the North Pole, He Lived in Turkey

So, let's start with the basics. Saint Nicholas was indeed a real person. He was a bishop, born to a Greek family, and he lived in the 4th century in Myra (present-day Turkey). That's pretty much all we can say for sure. The rest is a mishmash of historical fragments and folktales, according to Bruce David Forbes, a professor of religious studies at Morningside College in Iowa, and the author of *Christmas: A Candid History*.

Some examples of these folktales include Nicholas being jailed for starting a fist fight at a conference of bishops, being imprisoned and tortured in persecution, and being born to wealthy parents who died from the plague when he was young, leaving him a small fortune. His purported wealth and generosity are likely the basis of his reputation as a gift giver. One legend even tells of him stealthily visiting a home at night to leave gifts.

It Couldn't Have Been the Chimney

There are many versions of the story of Nicholas secretly giving money to the poor widower and his daughters. In one widely told version, he drops the money down their chimney, which obviously calls to mind how Santa Claus enters homes on Christmas Eve. The only problem with this is that the earliest examples of houses with chimneys aren't until the 12th century—nearly 800 years after Nicholas's death.

As Forbes recounts: "A widowed father had three daughters, and he tells them in tears that, because he has no money, he can't provide dowries for them to get married. They faced a future of slavery—or worse. Nicholas overhears this, and so he comes by in the dead of night and drops a bag of gold through the window, which allows one daughter to have a dowry. Another night, another bag of gold. On the third night, the father is lying in wait, and finds out that it's Nicholas. He says he wants to tell the world, but Nicholas says 'no.'"

It's believed that Nicholas died on December 6 in the year 343, at 73 years old. In the years following his death, his reputation grew, but not for the reasons you might think. Nowadays, he's known mostly as a generous gift giver. But in those early days, he was seen mainly as a kind of guardian angel and miracle worker. As his legend spread across Europe along with Christianity itself, he became the patron saint of seafarers, merchants, brewers, pawnbrokers, and travelers.

There are legends of Nicholas rescuing doomed ships, saving condemned men from execution, and multiplying grain stockpiles during a famine. In one especially gruesome legend, he resurrects three travelers who were murdered and dismembered by an evil innkeeper.

The First Santa-Centric Tourist Site

His stock had risen to the point that, more than seven centuries later, a group of Italian merchants in the town of Bari got a crazy idea. Just to be clear, this part is not a legend; this really happened.

As Forbes tells it, "You had this Italian community that was on hard times. And it was like the community council was trying to figure out: 'what can we do to improve our status?' They needed something that would draw people to the town. In those days, tourist attractions were usually religious. If you had relics of a saint, then people would make pilgrimages there, and you could get all kinds of income from that visit. They stole the relics, brought them back to Bari and built a Basilica around them. It was very successful because it was a port city, and this was about the time of the Crusades. So, Crusaders from all over Western Europe would come down to Italy and get on a boat to the Holy Land to fight. Bari was the perfect place, so they would go there, ask for a blessing of Saint Nicholas, and then go off on their Crusading."

The Basilica di San Nicola in Bari is still standing today, and it's an important pilgrimage destination for many.

Along with his name recognition came more and more people observing Saint Nicholas Day on December 6, the day marked to commemorate his death. Starting in the 12th century, certain French nuns began leaving sweets and gifts for children outside the homes of poor families on Saint Nicholas Day Eve. This was likely inspired by the legend of Saint Nicholas and the poor widower, and it's among the earliest known examples of giving gifts to children in Nicholas's name. It wasn't long before the idea of giving gifts to children around Saint Nicholas Day—all children, not just poor ones—caught on. Saint Nicholas markets even started popping up in early December, selling toys and candy.

Saint Nicholas Goes Norse, Gets a Horse

As his reputation continued spreading across Europe, it became mixed with local legends. For example, until the 14th century, his beard was usually pictured as dark. But he reminded some people of Odin, the white-bearded Norse god who, at the time of the winter solstice, rode across the sky at night on a white horse. Before long, Saint Nicholas was also pictured as having a long white beard, and riding a white horse.

In the Netherlands, the Feast of Sinterklaas on December 6th arose during the Middle Ages. The figure of Sinterklaas appeared in red bishop's robes and gave out gifts to children himself.

OUTSOURCING THE DISCIPLINE

Punishing children isn't exactly saintly. So in many regions, Saint Nicholas was said to have a servant or companion who did it for him. These characters include Knecht Ruprecht, Belsnickel, Krampus, Pere Fouettard, and Zwarte Piet.

He also began taking on traits of the elfin or witch-like deities from European folktales who rewarded good children, and punished naughty ones. Remember, up until now, his reputation was mostly as a guardian angel and miracle worker. But gradually, he also became known as a disciplinarian, and someone who knows whether you've been naughty or nice.

Up until the 16th century, Saint Nicholas had no association with Christmas. But then along came the Protestant Reformation. Protestants opposed devotion to saints, which meant that the popular Saint Nicholas Day celebration was off-limits. That didn't sit too well with many Nicholas-loving Protestants, so they came up with a plan to save Saint Nicholas Day while still playing by the rules.

Saint Nicholas's yearly gift-giving spree would move from December 5 (Saint Nicholas Day Eve) to Christmas Eve. At this point, Christmas is still not a major religious or cultural celebration, but a minor observance on the church calendar. Not only that, but also to keep Saint Nicholas out of the spotlight, his gift-giving duties would now be carried out by Christkindl (the Christ Child). That way, people could keep some familiar version of their popular celebration, but put the emphasis on the Christ Child instead of a saint.

The plan bombed. People missed Saint Nicholas. So, as a compromise, Saint Nicholas and the Christ Child would go around together on Christmas Eve. It was enough for Saint Nicholas and Christkindl to become intertwined and eventually, "Christkindl" was corrupted into the now familiar "Kris Kringle."

Within a century of the Reformation, Europeans began crossing the Atlantic and setting up colonies in the New World. The major shift from Saint Nicholas (or Sinterklass or Kris Kringle) into Santa Claus happened in America. More specifically, it happened in the Dutch settlement of New Amsterdam (now known as New York) where the Sinterklaas traditions lived on.

Starting in the early 1800s, the creation of the Santa Claus we all recognize today began happening rather quickly. Whereas legends and folktales spread slowly, and take on many regional differences, as we move into the 19th century, we see the effects of a method for quickly and widely spreading a single, common image: mass media.

In 1809, Washington Irving, published *A History of New York*. This satirical book, published under the pseudonym of Diedrich Knickerbocker, included references to Saint Nicholas that brought him one step closer to the figure we recognize today. For instance, he rode in a flying wagon pulled by horses. He slid down chimneys to deliver gifts into stockings hanging by the fire. One big difference, though, was that Irving described him visiting on New Year's Eve, not Christmas Eve.

"A Right Jolly Old Elf"

And then in 1823 a newspaper in New York published a poem on Christmas Eve . . . about Christmas Eve. It's a poem that went on to become one of the best known in the English language: "A Visit from Saint Nicholas" (or "'Twas the Night Before Christmas," as it's also commonly known). Its author, Clement Clarke Moore, picked up where Irving left off, but he made some big changes. He replaced the wagon with a sleigh, and the horses with reindeer, but the most dramatic change is something you may not have thought about before, even though it's right there in the poem: Saint Nicholas is an elf. He rides a miniature sleigh with eight tiny reindeer. He has a little round belly. Nobody had ever described Saint Nicholas like this before.

Four decades later, a political cartoonist named Thomas Nast was producing drawings for *Harper's Weekly* that would take the image of Santa one step further. The drawings varied quite a bit. Sometimes his suit looked like the one we know today; other times it looked more like long johns. Sometimes he had pointed ears or other physical features that suggested he was some kind of mythical figure.

Nast was also the first to depict Santa Claus as living in the North Pole. And during this period, we see the first mentions of a Mrs. Santa Claus in an 1849 short story by John Rees.

Nast continued creating Santa illustrations until the 1890s. And in the decades that followed, other artists—notably, Norman Rockwell—would create their own images of Santa, but usually staying fairly close to the character envisioned by Irving, Moore, and Nast. It wasn't until the early 1930s that we saw the finishing touches put on the image of Santa.

An 1889 illustration of Santa Claus from Thomas Nast. LIBRARY OF CONGRESS

The Claus That Refreshes

Haddon Sundblom was a commercial artist who created paintings for well-known brands. Starting in 1931, and continuing for 30 years, Sundblom would produce one or two annual Santa paintings for Coca-Cola. Because of Coca-Cola's massive advertising reach—in the form of billboard ads, magazine and newspaper ads, in-store displays, posters, figurines, and other collectibles—this single image spread quickly across the world, and became more or less the "official" Santa Claus: a full-sized adult man, and fully human, with no mythical physical features.

Considering that Sundblom put the finishing touches on Santa Claus starting in 1931, that means that the exact Santa we all recognize today is only a bit over 90 years old. Imagine that: there are people alive today who are older than Santa Claus himself!

But when we say that Sundblom put the "finishing touches" on Santa, that doesn't necessarily mean we're done with him yet. Given his dramatic transformation from bishop to magical gift giver, and given how his story is one of constant evolution over a 1,700-year span, there's every reason to expect that he'll continue to change as time goes on.

Did You Know?

James Edgar, owner of Edgar's Department Store in Brockton, Massachusetts, is credited as the first department store Santa. Edgar began making appearances in his store dressed as Santa starting in 1890.

CHAPTER 10

ANIMATED TV CHRISTMAS SPECIALS

The Golden Age of the 1960s

For generations of TV viewers, the word "SPECIAL," spinning around to a frenzied bongo-drum beat and horn section, meant one thing only: regularly scheduled programming on TV tonight was out the window. Tonight would bring a special presentation of an animated Christmas special.

Prime-time animated Christmas specials are one of our newer traditions, and they really are a bona fide tradition. They often involve the entire family arranging to be in the same place at the same time. They bring a sense of nostalgia and connection to the past. And like any tradition, there's an element of ritual.

When you think of the classic animated Christmas specials, a small handful come to mind immediately, ones like *Frosty the Snowman*, *A Charlie Brown Christmas*, and *Rudolph the Red-Nosed Reindeer* (see Chapter 13). They've aired in prime time every year for almost 60 years now. And what do they all have in common? They were all produced in the 1960s: 1962 to 1969 to be exact, a sort of golden age of Christmas animation.

With animation being what it is today, one would think we'd be knocking out modern classics left and right. But so far, nothing has quite caught on like that small number of gems from the 1960s. Why? Well, it's a combination of an animation industry that was undergoing some important changes around that time, clever content and marketing strategy, and the power of ritual and tradition.

Oh, Magoo—You've Done Scrooge Again

It all starts in 1962. Even though television was a mature medium by then, and even though Christmas-themed animated movie shorts had been recycled as TV content, no one had yet come around to producing an animated Christmas program specifically for television. "If there is a golden era of Christmas animated specials, it would have to start with *Mr. Magoo's Christmas Carol* in 1962, because it was the first Christmas animated special made specifically for television." So says Christmas TV expert Joanna Wilson, the author of several books on the subject, including *'Tis the Season TV*.

"There was animation at Christmas on television before *Mr. Magoo*," Wilson continues, "but it was made by Walt Disney for *Walt Disney Presents*, his weekly television show, and it was mostly recycled film shorts that he had already released into theaters."

Mr. Magoo's Christmas Carol is a musical adaptation of the classic Charles Dickens story. But why Mr. Magoo? According to Wilson, "They were looking to create complex stories that were appealing to everybody who might be sitting in front of the television set—that included children and parents and grandchildren."

You see this today with animated movies; the studios realize that parents will be watching with their children, so they'll throw in jokes and references the adults will get, and cast celebrities that adults will appreciate to voice the characters. *Mr. Magoo* was already a popular children's cartoon that began airing two years earlier (and the character had existed in theatrical shorts going back to 1949). *A Christmas Carol* was a well-known story, of course. And Jim Backus, who voiced Mr. Magoo, was already very familiar to adults from his extensive work on radio, movies, and television. Throw in some very high-quality music written by a team of Broadway composers, and you've got the perfect recipe to attract a wide viewership. Audiences and critics alike consider this a holiday classic.

But why did it take until the early 1960s for any of this to happen? "There were several conditions that made it conducive to write at that time," Wilson explains. "One was, the animation industry was changing; [throughout] the 1930s, 40s, and 50s, animation was dominated by big, Hollywood-studio animation companies. A lot of animators grew up working in these big studios and began to break off and make their own independent animation studios. Television was actually an expanding medium—animation was starting to pop up in the 50s, in commercials, and Hanna-Barbera began making original cartoons just for television in the late 50s and early 60s. So new content was being made just for television; [it wasn't] just recycled old film shorts [that] were being shown. And because new animation was coming into television, sponsors were willing [to support it], and that was an important thing that brought Christmas animation in."

A New TV Genre Is Born

And so, for the remainder of that decade, the major networks introduced new Christmas specials in prime time every year or two, following the proven formula of well-known characters, celebrity voice talent, and original music. Then 1964 brought the debut of *Rudolph the Red-Nosed Reindeer*, with Burl Ives as the narrator.

A Charlie Brown Christmas (see below) aired the following year. It didn't include any celebrity voice talent, but it did include a rather bold addition—a sophisticated jazz soundtrack by Vince Guaraldi. *How the Grinch Stole Christmas* arrived the year after that, with Boris Karloff as the narrator and that unforgettable song, "You're a Mean One, Mr. Grinch," which was sung by none other than Thurl Ravenscroft, who you may know better as the original voice of Tony the Tiger.

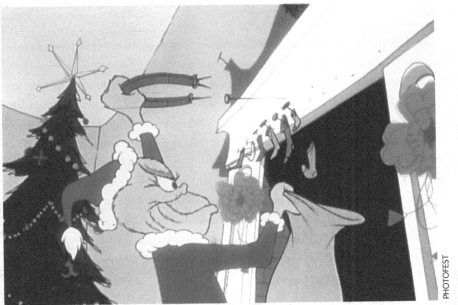

And we close out the decade with 1969's *Frosty the Snowman*, narrated by Jimmy Durante.

Of course, this wasn't the end of Christmas animation for TV, not by a long shot. Wilson observes, "Through the 70s and into the 80s, there's an explosion in Christmas animation. This also has a lot to do with the success of these first five that we mentioned. Now suddenly, other animators and animation companies are seeing, 'Wow, there's a market here. We can actually create Christmas animation, too.' And everybody did; every studio made at least one Christmas special, often more than that."

The 1970s brought us the stop-motion animation specials *Santa Claus Is Coming to Town* and *The Year Without a Santa Claus*, both of which were produced by Rankin/Bass, the same studio that made *Rudolph* and *Frosty*; they'd end up making a total of 19 Christmas programs.

The 1980s brought us a veritable Toys R Us catalog of programming, with specials centered around Pac-Man, the Cabbage Patch Kids, the Masters of the Universe, the Care Bears, and a whole lot more.

But what all of those specials have in common is that they're no longer aired by major networks in prime time, while those five specials from the golden age still are. (Even when *A Charlie Brown Christmas* made the move to the Apple TV+ streaming service, PBS stepped up to continue the special's annual tradition of airing on network television.) It's true that *Mr. Magoo's Christmas Carol* took a hiatus for a little while, but it's back now. *Rudolph* has aired in prime time annually since 1964, making it the longest-running Christmas TV special of all time.

A Moment of Family Togetherness, and Now a Word from Our Sponsor

But why? All of these programs are readily available on DVD. Audiences can watch them whenever they want. And yet, we still make time to watch them as scheduled programming. Surprisingly, the number of people doing that is on the rise, and it all comes back to that sense of nostalgia and ritual.

"I hear people repeat to me all the time," says Wilson, "that they make a special effort to watch it just how they watched it when they were children, which is when it airs on TV, broadcast with the commercials. That's still something that people feel nostalgic about when it comes to Christmas entertainment; they want to watch *Rudolph* with the commercials when it airs on TV. They want to watch *Charlie Brown* when it airs on TV."

In other words, maybe it's not just the show itself but also everything that goes with it. The sense of anticipation of a shared experience with people we love, the rare privilege of staying up past your bedtime and making special snacks to eat while watching it. We want to return to that again and again. And so we do.

Good Grief, Charlie Brown, You're a Christmas TV Legend

It's 1965, and we're in an office at the CBS headquarters building in New York City. (And since it's 1965, there's probably all kinds of wood paneling and cigarette smoke and thin-lapeled suits in our scene.) It's an urgent meeting of network executives to do a little bit of quality assurance and, if need be, a little emergency strategizing.

You see, for weeks now, they've been promoting a major network event, a prime-time special unlike anything that had ever been aired before. The only problem was they hadn't actually seen it yet. In fact, hardly anyone had. The whole project had been on an absurdly short timeline, the kind where even if everything went exactly right, the whole thing wouldn't come together until the very last second, and that last second was fast approaching. So here were the network executives, just one week before their major prime-time special is about to air, and they're about to sit down and watch the finished product for the first time.

"This will be the worst Christmas play ever."

And if that weren't enough pressure, right on the other side of the door to this office, out in the lobby, is a gaggle of journalists and critics—because as soon as the executives finished watching it, these people were going to come into the office for a private screening and then go off to publish the reviews in the likes of Time Magazine and other major publications. The executives finish watching, and they aren't happy. They thought it was flat and disjointed, confusing in some spots. The producers were convinced that they had failed, and that the project was a flop, and there just wasn't enough time to do anything about it.

But of course, they hadn't failed. It wasn't a flop. The critical acclaim came pouring in. And on December 9, 1965, one half of all the televisions in America were tuned to CBS to get into the Christmas spirit and to see a beloved set of comic-strip characters brought to life in this animated special.

This TV event was, of course, A Charlie Brown Christmas, one of the most beloved, enduring, and—for many reasons—unlikely successes in Christmas-television history.

PHOTOFEST

The story of how everything came together sounds like something out of an old-fashioned backstage comedy. To start with, "Peanuts" had been a popular syndicated newspaper comic strip since 1950. In April 1965, the "Peanuts" characters (including Snoopy, Lucy, Linus, Schroeder, and of course Charlie Brown) appeared on the cover of Time Magazine, securing their status as American icons. Several months later, another American icon—Coca-Cola— approached the McCann Erickson ad agency in New York. They were interested in sponsoring an animated Christmas special. John Allen at McCann Erickson reached out to producer Lee Mendelson, who had recently been shopping around a documentary that he produced about Charles Schultz and Peanuts.

"Due to the shortage of time, we'll get right to work."

As Benjamin Clark, curator of the Charles Schulz Museum in Santa Rosa, California, tells it, "[Mendelson] basically agreed to Coca-Cola, saying, 'Yes, we have an animated Christmas special for you.' And then he immediately hangs up the phone, calls up Charles Schultz, and says, 'How quick can we put together an animated special?'"

The first big hurdle to clear was that Coca-Cola needed an outline by the following Monday. "And this was late in the week," Clark continues, "and after [hanging up on Coca-Cola] and [calling] Schulz, [Mendelson] drove up here to Santa Rosa. And they sat down and outlined it in a single day and sent it off to Coca-Cola. And they said, 'Let's do it.'"

After they had an outline, and then a script, they needed an animator. Schulz suggested that they hire Bill Melendez, whom he had worked with on a Peanuts-themed ad for the Ford Motor Company. Melendez agreed to come on board, but he knew that it was going to be really difficult to pull it off within the short timeline. And there were a couple of unique complications with animating these particular characters.

"It's hard to get Charlie Brown to turn and keep the proportions of his head right," notes Clark. "And their arms are so short, you know, they can't lift anything above their heads. So it was tough, and they had to get kind of creative on some of those things."

"One of the first things to ensure a good performance is strict attention to the director."

In addition to that, Schulz insisted on using real child actors, not adults, to voice the characters, which was very different from the standard of the day. "Bill Melendez would be there at the studio feeding kids their lines," Clark recounts with a chuckle. "Bill is originally from Mexico, and spoke English with a Mexican accent, and some of the kids would begin to imitate that accent as he's feeding them their line. And it would get everybody laughing, and they'd have to try to have the kid repeat it again."

And speaking of voicing the characters, you hear the voice of Bill Melendez himself in the special, although that wasn't the original intention. "The voicing of Snoopy—who does not speak, but he kind of growls and grumbles and expresses surprise—is actually voiced by Bill Melendez," Clark reveals. "And those were recorded just as placeholders while they were working through the animation and trying to figure out these things. And Schulz heard it and said, 'Oh, yeah, that's great. That's perfect.'"

Despite the absurdly short schedule and high pressure, the team pulled it off. According to Clark, "From greenlight to delivery was almost six months on the nose. They said they actually delivered it a week before it aired."

Which brings us back to that fateful meeting at the CBS building, just a week before the airdate, where network executives were convinced that they were walking into a disaster. You can kind of see where they were coming from: In the first place, while there is a central story of Charlie Brown producing a Christmas play, the plot does feel like it's kind of all over the place.

A lot of it's derived from the strip," explains Clark. "It's in these brief little episodes, and you get these little arcs within it. And that works because the comic strip works."

"I know nobody likes me. Why do we have to have a holiday season to emphasize it?"

And for a children's special and a Christmas special, the show goes into some pretty odd places. Within its 25-minute runtime, the special touches on depression, commercialism, and that iconic Linus moment, a Bible verse, which CBS was apparently not very happy about. And floating over all of it is a very 1960s jazz soundtrack from Vince Guaraldi, who Mendelson was a big fan of. A lot of that music isn't even especially Christmas-sounding, and apparently Schultz was against using it. "It should not have worked, but it did," observes Clark.

The initial success may have been based on the popularity of the characters and a chance to experience them in a new way. Or based on the popularity of Christmas specials in general, and the scarcity of them at the time—we're swimming in content nowadays, but back in the 60s, there were just a small handful of television channels, and a new animated prime-time special was a major cultural event. That initial success translated into another prime-time airing the following year. And the year after that.

"All I want is what's coming to me. All I want is my fair share."

Eventually, nostalgia became part of the reason we continue watching. A Charlie Brown Christmas has aired in prime time every year since 1965. That almost came to an end in 2020, when Apple TV+ became the home for all Peanuts animation. The original announcement that A Charlie Brown Christmas would stream exclusively on Apple TV+ led to an enormous uproar from the public; it wound up airing on PBS, where it has become an annual fixture. In an age when we can watch the special whenever we want, and through a variety of methods, it really says something about the power of nostalgia and tradition that, around Christmas time, appointment television viewing is still a thing.

Notes Clark, "Even Schulz's wife, Jeanne Schultz, said, 'Well, it's nice it's going to be on TV, so people like me who are kind of old-fashioned about these things can still watch it.'"

CHAPTER 11

THE NUTCRACKER

The Greatest Russian Christmas Story America Ever Told

Hearing just the first few notes of "Dance of the Sugar Plum Fairy," you're transported to a world of opulent spectacle: a fancy holiday party, a Christmas tree that magically grows to dizzying heights, a mouse king and a life-size nutcracker who comes to life, sugarplum fairies and dancing snowflakes, a land of sweets, and exotic dances from exotic characters from all over the world.

The unmistakable music and imagery of *The Nutcracker* is as much a part of our Christmas landscape as Santa Claus himself, and attending a live performance of the ballet is a cherished annual tradition for families all across the country. Whether you live in a large city or a small town, there's probably at least one production of *The Nutcracker* being staged near you.

Made in Moscow

Of course, it wasn't always that way. The vast majority of the Christmas traditions we observe today in America got their start somewhere else, usually England and Europe. *The Nutcracker* also got its start somewhere else—Russia, in this case—but the interesting part is that it didn't become a Christmas tradition until it reached America.

As far as Christmas traditions go, this is one of the newest ones we have. We're talking very new here. And it's all the result of a chain reaction starting with the formation of the Soviet Union, changing cultural tastes in America, and a little help along the way from Walt Disney.

Our story begins at the Imperial Mariinsky Theatre in St. Petersburg, Russia. It's 1892, and we're right in Russia's golden age of classical ballet. Composer Peter Tchaikovsky had already written the scores for *Sleeping Beauty* and *Swan Lake*, so the director of the Imperial Theatre has commissioned him to write a new score. It would be for a ballet based on the story *The Nutcracker and the Mouse King*, written by the German author E. T. A. Hoffman in 1816. It was revised and translated into French by Alexandre Dumas in 1844—that's the same Alexandre Dumas who wrote *The Three Musketeers* and *The Count of Monte Cristo*.

The story follows the basic plot of the Dumas adaptation, in which a young girl named Clara receives a beautiful nutcracker as a gift on Christmas Eve. She falls asleep with the nutcracker in her arms, and as the clock strikes midnight, strange and magical things start happening.

A Sugarplum Flop

Believe it or not, despite all of its festive trappings, that original production in 1892 was not considered a success.

"*The Nutcracker* in Russia received mixed reviews," reveals Jennifer Fisher, a self-described "Nutcracker-ologist." A professor of dance history at the University of California, Irvine, Fisher is the author of *Nutcracker Nation: How an Old World Ballet Became a Tradition in the New World.*

"There were a lot of complaints about *The Nutcracker,*" Fisher continues. "The major ballerina role wasn't until very late in the evening, and it had children in it who didn't behave well on stage. There were, in fact, complaints about Tchaikovsky, which are hard for us to believe. Important music was not yet common to be used with ballet, and so the critics found it very complex on the ear. One of them called it 'undanceable music.'"

Tchaikovsky received detailed instructions from the choreographer for writing the score, such as "The stage is empty. 8 bars of mysterious and tender music" or "The Christmas tree becomes huge. 48 bars of fantastic music with a grandiose crescendo." As Jennifer Fisher explains, back then it was common for ballet composers to write music "by the yard" like this.

And even though it's hard to imagine *The Nutcracker* as anything but a Christmas story, the emphasis on the Christmasy aspects would come much later.

According to Fisher, "The Christmas aspect was simply not that important. There was a party—the same way there would be a party in the Czar's palace, and it happened to have a Christmas tree in it—but the tree wasn't that important. You've watched American productions where Christmas is foregrounded, whereas it would be backgrounded in their production."

Christmas wasn't the dominant cultural holiday in Russia: That would be Orthodox Easter. Only when it was produced in America would Christmas be placed front and center. And even though there would be feature productions of *The Nutcracker* in Russia, it never really caught on. It wasn't until *The Nutcracker* was produced outside of Russia that it would really catch fire.

Bring Me Your Tired, Your Weary, Your Christmas Ballets

With the formation of the Soviet Union in the early 20th century, many Russians fled their homeland, bringing along *The Nutcracker*. "*The Nutcracker* emigrates slowly," says Fisher, "and it does so with the Russians who left the Soviet Union early in the 20th century. The Russians are dispersing with fragments of *The Nutcracker* and taking it on tour with them."

The first complete performance of *The Nutcracker* outside of Russia was in England in 1934. Before a full ballet production was ever performed here in America, Americans got their first taste of Tchaikovsky's score in Disney's 1940 animated movie *Fantasia*, which featured animated sequences set to the music. *Fantasia* is often thought to have made classical music more popular in America and gave the music of *The Nutcracker*, in particular, a big boost.

"It puts the ballet and its aesthetics and its complex music into animated form," Fisher observes. "I maintain that this allowed Americans to enter this world of high art. These aesthetic aspects really take you into the world of ballet. So maybe audiences that weren't used to going to the ballet, it allowed them, I think, to get closer to that tradition."

From Holiday Placeholder to Annual Tradition

Four years later, the ballet was performed in its entirety for the first time in America in San Francisco. Adds Fisher, "And that was accidental, really. The opera house in San Francisco happened to be dark during the holidays. The Ballets Russes, a few of these Russians, happened to be touring in San Francisco, and they advised the artistic director of the San Francisco Ballet, William Christensen, 'You should do a *Nutcracker*. It has a Christmas theme, and there's a Christmas tree in the first act.' So William Christensen stages a *Nutcracker*, and they don't do it the next year in San Francisco, but the year after, they do start to do it [annually] because they realize that it's a great time of year."

In 1954, the New York City Ballet put on its first production staged by George Balanchine, who's known as the father of American ballet. That production became highly influential, and by the 1960s, *The Nutcracker* was being produced annually all across the country. "One of the major things that happens along the way," Fisher notes, "is that Americans start to make *The Nutcracker* look like themselves." The real beauty of *The Nutcracker* is how it can be endlessly adapted.

Five Ways to Watch The Nutcracker Without Leaving Your House

If you can support your local dance troupe by buying tickets to their annual production of The Nutcracker, *that's a win for both you and them. But if you can't make it to a live performance this Christmas, you've got a range of options:*

Nutcracker *(1986): Carroll Ballard* (The Black Stallion) *directs this big-screen adaptation featuring the Pacific Northwest Ballet's original production. This film version is probably best known for the memorable production design by legendary children's-book author and illustrator Maurice Sendak* (Where the Wild Things Are).

The Nutcracker *(1992): Following the release of the smash-hit, Christmas-set family comedies* Home Alone *(1990) and* Home Alone 2: Lost in New York *(1992), 12-year-old former ballet dancer Macaulay Culkin was arguably the biggest star in Hollywood. Given his past successes in toe shoes and in holiday stories, it was probably a no-brainer to feature him in the title role alongside members of the New York City Ballet.*

A Nutcracker Christmas *(2016): When Hallmark Channel and Hallmark Movies & Mysteries crank up their 24/7 Christmas-movie marathons each year, this love story often enters the mix—Amy Acker stars as a former ballerina who reenters the world of dance when her young niece gets cast in a production of* The Nutcracker. *There's plenty of ballet footage (and, of course, Acker's character finds love with a hunky choreographer).*

The Nutcracker and the Four Realms *(2018): This big-budget fantasy from Disney uses the E. T. A. Hoffman story as a springboard for an elaborate tale of warring factions in a fairy-tale kingdom, but the film does wisely pause the action to allow prima ballerina Misty Copeland to perform.*

Dance Dreams: Hot Chocolate Nutcracker *(2020): This spirited documentary takes us behind the scenes of Debbie Allen's annual holiday extravaganza. It's a powerful and heartwarming look at the blending of the old and the new, and how traditions can evolve and expand with the input of new communities and new artists.*

Holiday tip: Do not, under any circumstances, subject yourself to 2010's The Nutcracker: The Untold Story *(aka* The Nutcracker in 3D). *From Tim Rice's clunky hip-hop orchestrations to the inexplicable decision to add Albert Einstein as a character (played by Nathan Lane, no less), this legendary flop is a ten-sugarplum pileup of bad decisions.*

Hawaiian ballet companies produce hula Nutcrackers. There are urban Nutcrackers, hip-hop Nutcrackers, drag Nutcrackers, and in San Francisco, there's even a dance-along Nutcracker, where the audience is encouraged to attend in costume and get in on the action.

Because of all of that, *The Nutcracker* is now the most popular ballet in the world, ever, and it accounts for between 30% and 90% of the annual income for ballet companies that produce it. It's a meteoric rise for a ballet that wasn't even considered important, and more or less languished for more than 50 years, before becoming a wide-scale annual tradition within a couple of decades. Aside from being a spectacular show, it's also a fascinating example of an invented tradition, one that caught hold because it fit in with the existing holiday traditions and attitudes of the new home to which it immigrated. You could say it's an immigrant success story, which makes it uniquely American in its own right.

CHAPTER 12

CLASSIC CHRISTMAS MOVIES

They're Not Just for Summer Anymore

Christmas movies couldn't have become a Christmas tradition without television. After all, it's hard to imagine theaters running the same Christmas movies each year during the season, and families having a tradition of all going to the movie theater to watch those movies together. No, it took television to create the notion of the "Christmas movie" as we know it. That probably sounds inconceivable, given that many of the most beloved Christmas movies began their life as theatrical releases, sometimes predating television by decades.

But the story for some of those movies is that they were critical and commercial disappointments—or middling successes at best—as theatrical releases. They often involved head-scratching studio decisions, such as being released during the summer. Is *It's a Wonderful Life* considered a classic due to its undeniable greatness? Or did a quirk of American copyright law lend a helping hand? It flopped at the box office in 1947. But when its copyright lapsed in the early 1970s and the film fell into public domain, it wallpapered TV stations, introducing a new generation of fans to a movie that had essentially fallen between the cracks. Not only that, but the movie transformed from merely a movie depicting Christmas to a "Christmas movie," one that provides a shared experience year after year for families and friends.

Similarly, *A Christmas Story* did reasonably well when it played theaters in 1983, and began attaining cult status on VHS and HBO, but it was Ted Turner who implanted the comedy into the American consciousness by taking a page from the history of *It's a Wonderful Life* and airing 24-hour *Christmas Story* marathons on his cable channels.

The small screen played an essential role in elevating those movies to cult status. It plays a similar role in keeping other classic Christmas movies in the zeitgeist, and for keeping alive the surprisingly new notion of a Christmas movie. Friends and loved ones gathering together to watch movies like *It's a Wonderful Life*, *A Christmas Story*, *Christmas in Connecticut*, and *Miracle on 34th Street* on broadcast television, streaming, DVD, or even at a local repertory theater have become part of many Americans' holiday traditions. Here's a look behind these beloved films and the cultural foothold they enjoy every December.

A Christmas Story

The tale of a young Ralphie (played by Peter Billingsley) and his seemingly impossible quest to get a Red Ryder BB gun for Christmas has taken on a life beyond itself: Besides the annual 24-hour marathon, it's spawned merchandise (leg-lamp Christmas ornaments! "Oh, Fudge" ice cream!) and stage adaptations and sequels. The house in the movie was made into a museum, and there's even a bronze statue of Flick licking the flagpole at the Indiana Welcome Center.

Actor Scott Schwartz, who played Flick, remembers, "The first time we shot it was 12 and a half hours from beginning to end for the whole thing. It was hysterical. You know, we had hand warmers and leg warmers, and we had battery-operated socks and long johns. I mean, it was a riot. It was freezing, but it was a riot." Alas, he continues, "Unfortunately, due to some not-too-good people at the lab up there in Canada, they underdeveloped the film, and we had to do it again. And we did a good job. We cut an hour off. We did it in 11 and a half hours."

For a film that has become such a minted family classic, it comes from decidedly adult origins. Writer Jean Shepherd (who also narrates the film) began publishing reminiscences from his childhood as a series of stories in *Playboy* magazine, and director Bob Clark—whose previous foray into holiday movies had been the influential slasher classic *Black Christmas* (1974)—attained the clout to make *A Christmas Story* only after his smash success with the low-budget sex comedy *Porky's* and its sequels.

One aspect of *A Christmas Story* that really appeals to people is the sense of nostalgia that the movie evokes—not just the nostalgia of having grown up watching the movie, but also the nostalgia for a bygone era depicted within the film. So it's interesting to point out that we don't know for sure when the movie is supposed to take place. There is a reference to the movie version of *The Wizard of Oz*, so that means it's set no earlier than 1939. The soundtrack includes Bing Crosby's version of *Santa Claus Is Coming to Town*, which came out in 1943. So it's set in a sort of amorphous period of late 30s to early 40s. But there's that sense of timelessness about it: The story of the young boy and that one special Christmas gift he dreams about is something anyone who celebrates Christmas can relate to, regardless of time or place.

And what's it like for Schwartz to be a living, breathing Christmas tradition? "I celebrate Hanukkah, which is very funny. You know, I'm in an American iconic Christmas film and I'm Jewish, but I see how people react, and I see what their feelings are and how they project care and love for all of us. I think it's cool to be a part of something that people 30 years later still want to watch. It's like we're a part of their family."

It's a Wonderful Life

The beloved tale of George Bailey—and how his attempted suicide (and the intervention of a guardian angel) makes him appreciate the many lives he's touched—began life as a short story, "The Greatest Gift," by Philip Van Doren Stern. When Van Doren Stern couldn't find a publisher for his holiday tale of redemption, he sent it out in Christmas cards, one of which landed on the desk of director Frank Capra.

Looking for a project to launch his new production company, Liberty Films, Capra seized upon this tale of a small-town hero who spent his life making sacrifices for others, and the way that those others repay the favor in our hero's darkest hour. Capra and the film's star, James Stewart, were both returning to Hollywood after World War II—Capra made propaganda films for the US government, while Stewart flew missions with the Army Air Force.

"There's a tendency for us to look back and think, 'Oh, we used to be so innocent, we used to be so naïve,'" notes Alonso Duralde, author of *Have Yourself a Movie Little Christmas*. "But you have to remember, this is right on the heels of World War II. So people had lost loved ones, people had been hearing news on the radio, in the newspapers, every day about bombings and refugees.

The scene in It's a Wonderful Life *where Clarence saves George from jumping off a bridge was shot on a 90-degree day. Jimmy Stewart is visibly sweating in the scene.*

We had collectively gone through this tragedy. And it's not even Capra's first film about a guy who attempts to commit suicide on Christmas Eve—that would be *Meet John Doe* with Gary Cooper and Barbara Stanwyck."

And while there's so much from *It's a Wonderful Life* that has entered the culture—Zuzu's petals, the song "Buffalo Gals," the idea that "every time a bell rings, an angel gets his wings"—the film made another important, if often unsung, contribution. Prior to *It's a Wonderful Life*, filmmakers used corn flakes (painted white) as fake snow, and since they were so noisy when actors stepped on them, dialogue had to be recorded separately.

Capra and his team completely revolutionized fake snow for the film, using a combination of Ivory soap flakes, chipped ice, and a substance called "foamite," which is similar to the stuff you find in fire extinguishers today. So when you see Hallmark actors in a Christmas movie, pretending to shiver in the heat of Vancouver in August, remember that the fake snow falling all around them was first developed for this Christmas classic.

Miracle on 34th Street

When is a Christmas movie not a Christmas movie? In the case of *Miracle of 34th Street*, it's when a sentimental comedy about Santa Claus gets released in the summer of 1947.

"Darryl Zanuck, who ran 20th Century Fox in the 1940s, didn't think that enough people went to the movies at Christmas time. He was much more interested in trying to get a summer audience to attend," says Duralde. "And the advertising does not in any way say this is a movie about Santa Claus, and it takes place at Christmas. The film's original trailer follows somebody going around the Fox lot and talking about the film with different studio contract players at the time. They all

say how much they love the movie, but one of them describes it as a comedy, another one was moved by the drama, and someone else talks up the romance. Santa Claus is never mentioned."

As batty as the idea sounds, the gamble paid off for 20th Century Fox: *Miracle on 34th Street* was a smash success when it hit theaters in June. It made a star out of young Natalie Wood and earned a Best Supporting Actor Oscar for Edmund Gwenn for his portrayal of Santa Claus. Wood plays Susan Walker, a young girl who has been raised to be rational and pragmatic by her mother Doris (Maureen O'Hara), who works at Macy's. When the Santa hired for the store's annual parade turns up drunk, Kris Kringle (Gwenn) steps in and winds up changing the lives of the Walkers, and even the way Macy's does business, over the course of one magical Christmas season.

The ongoing impact of *Miracle* extends beyond its success as a film. It had the interesting side effect of making the Macy's Thanksgiving Day Parade the national institution it is today. While the parade itself had been around since 1924, it was strictly a New York thing for the first 20-odd years of its existence. The earliest TV broadcasts were just on local stations. But that iconic opening scene of *Miracle on 34th Street* brought the parade to the masses, and networks started broadcasting coverage nationally the year after the movie hit theaters.

"That's the actual 1946 Macy's Thanksgiving Day Parade at the beginning of the film," says Duralde. "They were given permission to shoot it, and Edmund Gwenn was, in fact, the Santa Claus of the parade that year."

Not only that, but it also inspired the real Macy's department store to hire "Kristine Kringle," who would direct shoppers to better deals at competing stores, just as Kris Kringle told Macy's shoppers in the movie to go to Gimbels.

Like *It's a Wonderful Life*, *Miracle on 34th Street* very much reflects its postwar moment. "There were children who knew more about the evils of the world than they probably should have, and the film gives us a child growing up in a cynical reality that has no room for fantasy," Duralde observes, which makes this the right movie for the right cultural moment. The film endures because, at its core, it's about a little girl who never got the chance to be a little girl, and how she discovers her childlike side through the magic of Christmas and the gift of a new friend. (That said, with the notable exception of the charming 1947 Lux Radio Theater adaptation, it's best to steer clear of the remakes.)

Christmas in Connecticut

World War II crosses paths with Christmas once again, and it's clear from the opening scene of *Christmas in Connecticut* that 1944 audiences had a sense of humor that had been shaped by several years of global conflict. The film is a breezy romantic comedy, but it opens with just two GIs surviving the sinking of a US troop ship.

One of those survivors, war hero Jefferson Jones (Dennis Morgan), is a big fan of lifestyle writer Elizabeth Lane (Barbara Stanwyck). Elizabeth is the Martha Stewart of the moment, writing an influential column about cooking, raising a baby, and tending to her beautiful Connecticut house. Trouble is, Elizabeth is a fraud—she's single, lives in a one-bedroom apartment in Manhattan, and lives entirely off food from the restaurant downstairs—but her boss wants Jefferson to be her guest for Christmas, requiring Elizabeth to come up with a house, a baby, and some cooking skills, fast.

Warner Brothers, the studio that made the movie, described it as a story of "finding the right man on the wrong honeymoon, when Santa Claus brings a bachelor girl a sweetheart, a husband, and two babies for Christmas." "There's a frantic level of wackiness," says Duralde, "what they call a slamming-doors farce, where people are coming in and out of rooms quickly, and you have to make sure that Person A doesn't see Person C or then Person B will be found out as a liar. There's a lot of moving parts and a lot of plates that have to be kept spinning."

Like *Miracle on 34th Street*, *Christmas in Connecticut* was a summer release that became a box-office hit—and like all the films mentioned above, it's a movie that became a seasonal perennial as television programmers looked for holiday fare to boost their December viewership.

Classic Christmas Movies **83**

CHAPTER 13

RUDOLPH, THE RED-NOSED REINDEER

An Underdog Story—But Not the One You Think

Everyone loves a good underdog story—and if that underdog story also happens to be a Christmas story, well, that's even better. There's one underdog story that's a Christmas favorite for lots of us: It's the tale of a little guy who always felt inferior. He was smaller and weaker than his peers, and he wasn't included in their games. But he would go on to leave an indelible mark on Christmas; you might even say a big, red, glowing mark. You know his name, of course: Robert.

You probably weren't expecting to hear that. But it perfectly describes Robert L. May, who created *Rudolph the Red-Nosed Reindeer*. And the story behind the story is almost as magical and endearing and triumphant as that of the little oddball who goes on to save Christmas. Maybe the name Robert May didn't go down in "his-tor-ree" like that of his famous character, but this much is clear: he changed Christmas forever.

"But do you recall . . ."

You know Rudolph from the song and the TV special (and more on them in a moment), but did you know that the character started out in a storybook? Don't feel bad if you didn't—the book was first published in 1939, and you can't buy a copy today. In fact, you could never buy a copy anywhere, because the original storybook was a promotional giveaway produced by the Montgomery Ward department store.

Year after year, Montgomery Ward gave out free books to children of holiday shoppers. But in 1939, the management decided to try to save money by producing its own book rather than buying them from booksellers. And that's where our story begins.

"All of the other reindeer / Used to laugh and call him names . . ."

Robert May was a copywriter for Montgomery Ward, living in Chicago. Educated at Dartmouth, a member of Phi Beta Kappa even, May had always had bigger dreams, like writing the great American novel. But he always had trouble fitting in.

According to Dartmouth archivist Peter Carini, "He was on the small side and didn't excel socially. A lot of his classmates had already found success, [as did] people who were close to him in age, like Theodore Geisel [better known as Dr. Seuss], who was Class of '25." May, meanwhile, was 35 years old, grinding out catalog descriptions of sweaters and dress shirts, all for a meager paycheck.

It was January 1939. All around Chicago, the Christmas decorations were coming down. That was just fine for Robert. He hadn't been feeling very festive—his wife Evelyn was dying of cancer, and his salary could barely cover the medical expenses. He was sinking into debt, all while raising a four-year-old daughter named Barbara. But one day, his boss called him into the office and asked him to come up with a story for the Christmas giveaway that year. The direction he was given was to write a story kind of like "Ferdinand the Bull."

"Then one foggy Christmas Eve . . ."

Robert decided that the animal should be a reindeer, because Barbara loved the reindeer exhibit at the Lincoln Park Zoo, and he wanted to do an underdog story. He was inspired when he saw the fog rolling off Lake Michigan, which made driving difficult and dim to the streetlights. So he put it all together and came up with a story of a red-nosed reindeer who was almost named Rollo, and then Reginald, before finally settling on Rudolph.

The next day, he marched into his boss's office and presented the idea. And as May himself would later write, the response he got was, "Can't you do any better than that?"

Says Carini, "His boss thought it was a terrible idea. He kind of scoffed at the idea of a reindeer, and he sent him back to rewrite it."

"As they shouted out with glee"

It's also been said that the boss didn't like the idea of a red nose because of its association with chronic alcoholism. This was the time when W. C. Fields was a household name, after all. "May, though, was really committed to this story and thought it was really good," Carini continues, "So he went to his friend Denver Gillen, who was an illustrator for Montgomery Ward and asked him to draw a mock-up for it. And he brought it back to his boss, who looked at it and had a completely different reaction once he could see it with the illustrations attached to the story. He was like, 'This is brilliant. This is great. We're gonna go with this.'"

May had the go-ahead to make the concept into a more finished version. And in July of that year, about a month before he finished the story, his wife Evelyn died. His boss offered to take the assignment off his plate, but as May would later write, he needed Rudolph then more than ever. He kept at it until the story was finished in August.

The story is told in rhyming verse and tells us the story you're mostly familiar with, but there are a couple of surprising details in the original. For example, on that stormy Christmas Eve, Santa and his reindeer attempt to make the deliveries anyway, despite the fog, and almost end up getting clipped by an airplane. And when Rudolph blushes, his whole body turns red. It's really a wonderful story. (And thank goodness for the internet, because you can find it online.)

That year, Montgomery Ward gave away about two and a half million copies of the book at their stores all across the country. The book was a big hit for Montgomery Ward, but it did relatively little for the workaday wordsmith behind it, who was still buried in debt. May was even approached by a publisher who wanted him to do a spoken-word recording of the story—but he couldn't, because Montgomery Ward held the copyright.

And then, something amazing happened. Something that could even be called a Christmas miracle.

"In 1947, Montgomery Ward decided they had had a good enough run with Rudolph," says Carini. "and they were going to discontinue using him. And May's boss asked that Montgomery Ward turn over the copyright of that story to May."

This is really unheard of, and there are conflicting accounts about why it even happened. Some say that Montgomery Ward was being big-hearted and wanted to help out May; others say that it was because they just didn't see the potential. More than six million kids already had the book, so what else could they do with it after that? Believe what you want, but May definitely saw the potential.

"Then how the reindeer loved him"

He even went to Disney with the idea of doing something with the character. Notes Carini, "Yeah, he did try to pitch it to Disney. They were not particularly interested at the time." It didn't matter. because it just so happened that his brother-in-law was Johnny Marks, a songwriter who specialized in Christmas songs.

You know "Rockin' Around the Christmas Tree"? "Holly Jolly Christmas"? "Silver and Gold"? Those are all his. Now these weren't just Christmas songs—these were *hit* Christmas songs. So Marks wrote the song, with a vocalist named Harry Brannon singing it originally. But in 1949, the singing cowboy himself, Gene Autry, recorded a version and it shot to number one on the charts.

"That generated two movies," recalls Carini. "A short that was done in the 40s and then the 1964 AniMagic TV special that we're all very familiar with." The piece from the 1940s is a cartoon from legendary animator Max Fleischer—best known for his "Popeye" and "Superman" shorts—that tells the story exactly as it's told in the storybook.

Did You Know?

Beginning in 1965, the year after the debut of the TV special, NBC aired an altered version of Rudolph with some of the original scenes deleted. At several times in the special, the prospector Yukon Cornelius tosses his pickaxe into the snow, and then licks it. The audience believes that he is searching for silver and gold, and can recognize them by their taste.

In fact, in the original version, Yukon is searching for an elusive peppermint mine, which he ultimately discovers outside of Santa's workshop in the final moments of the story. NBC never again aired that version, nor has CBS since taking over the special. However, the deleted scene is included in the DVD and Blu-Ray releases, and is easily found online.

Going Down in History . . . Over and Over and Over Again

Since Rudolph was one of the earliest, most successful, and most beloved Christmas TV specials, it's no surprise that producers are drawn to his red nose like a moth to a flame. Given the number of sequels and remakes he's spawned over the years, Rudolph is the gift that keeps on giving.

Rankin/Bass, the animation studio that created the 1964 original, returned to the character two more times: in 1976, with Rudolph's Shiny New Year, which pushed our hero beyond Christmas to December's other big holiday, and then in 1979 for the feature-length holiday crossover tale Rudolph and Frosty's Christmas in July. Another company completely unrelated to Rankin/Bass crafted their own sequel, using a location and characters invented for the 1964 TV special: 2001's Rudolph the Red-Nosed Reindeer and the Island of Misfit Toys, produced with computer animation rather than the stop-motion for which the original is so fondly remembered.

"The [TV special] is actually quite a different story," notes Carini. "The basic premise is the same, and the outcome is similar, but the [special] is much more in-depth and has a lot more characters." The show was first aired in 1964 on an NBC show called *The General Electric Fantasy Hour*, and since 1972, it's run every year on CBS, which makes it the longest-running Christmas TV special ever (see Chapter 10).

Robert May died a very wealthy man in 1976, and Rudolph remains one of the most enduring Christmas characters. Rudolph even appeared on a postage stamp in 2014, and the TV special has spawned sequels and has even been adapted into a stage musical.

PART III

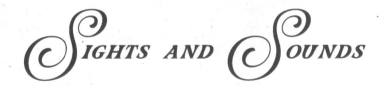

SIGHTS AND SOUNDS

The season is a wonderland of sights and sounds. Whether it's ancient carols, twinkling lights, or the greenery that decks the hall, these many sights and sounds create a uniquely Christmasy atmosphere of magic and enchantment. Each one became part of Christmas at a separate time in history, and with its own story to tell. Why were snow globes ever seen in operating rooms? How did a fateful mishap at a stationery store forever change the face of Christmas? And how do birds spread Christmas cheer? Read on to see some of our most familiar sights and sounds of the season in a new light.

CHAPTER 14

"JINGLE BELLS"

"Oh, what fun"

Go to your favorite internet search engine and enter "1898 Edison Jingle Bells." What you'll hear is an old wax cylinder from the turn of the 20th century, featuring the Edison Male Quartette. They put out a record called *Sleigh Ride Party*, which featured short skits and songs, including the familiar one you just found online. At the time this record was made, "Jingle Bells"—as the song is now known—was only a few decades old, making this among the earliest surviving recordings of the song.

Exactly 100 years after "Jingle Bells" was first published, Bobby Helms released his rockabilly homage: "Jingle Bell Rock." That song has become a Christmas classic in its own right.

Now search for "Gemini 6 Jingle Bells." It's 67 years later, and astronauts Wally Schirra and Tom Stafford were the astronauts on NASA's Gemini 6. They made history by completing the first rendezvous of a spacecraft that had a live crew onboard with another spacecraft. But they also made history in another way: They smuggled a harmonica and sleigh bells onto the craft, and on December 16, 1965, Schirra contacted Mission Control to say that he had detected an object, possibly a satellite,

Wally Schirra, one of the Gemini 6 astronauts responsible for making "Jingle Bells" the first song ever broadcast from space. PHOTOFEST

about to reenter the Earth's atmosphere, and he was going to try to patch through a signal to Mission Control. And then, taking everyone by surprise, Schirra and Stafford pulled out their smuggled instruments to play a rendition of "Jingle Bells."

Not only was it a truly epic prank, but it also marks the first song ever to be broadcast from space. That's a pretty big achievement for a little song that very well could have gone the way of similar music of the time, lost to history or hidden in the pages of obscure anthologies. "Jingle Bells" is synonymous with Christmas, even though it never mentions Christmas. It's one of the first Christmas songs children learn. It's an evergreen beginners' piano piece. And it brings to mind those idealized and sentimental images of snow and fun that go hand-in-mitten with the season.

But there's much, *much* more to the story of "Jingle Bells" than you ever could have imagined. Tracing the story of one of the best known Christmas songs will take us through minstrel halls, "sleigh-ride culture," and a feud between two American towns, each insisting on being the true birthplace of the song—a feud that's still going on today.

"In the frosty air"

According to a plaque in Medford, Massachusetts, a man named James Lord Pierpont wrote the song that would go on to become known as "Jingle Bells" in a tavern there in 1850. Kyna Hamill, director of core curriculum at Boston University and a reference volunteer for the Medford Historical Society and Museum, begs to differ. "1850 is absolutely incorrect. He is not even in Medford in 1850. The song doesn't get copyrighted until 1857," she notes.

Stick a pin in the place-of-authorship debate for the moment, and let's investigate the author himself. James Lord Pierpont: Confederate soldier, son of an abolitionist minister, uncle to the financier JP Morgan. He was, to say the least, an interesting fellow.

"James, I think, was probably a bit of a disappointment," says Hamill. "He moved around all the time. He had many, many, many different professions. He abandoned his children in 1867. I think they ended up having to go live with an uncle in Troy, New York. He just lived for himself."

Pierpont was one of those guys who's not quite what you'd call an entrepreneur, but more like the kind who would find almost any way he could to make a buck. He ran off to join the California Gold Rush, did random work as a photographer, wrote songs for the Confederacy, and in 1857, he published a song titled "The One-Horse Open Sleigh."

According to Hamill, "It is a song that was written specifically for a Boston minstrel troupe." And this is where things get uncomfortable. Minstrel shows were a form of theater where white men, playing both male and female roles, would darken their skin with makeup to perform burlesque versions of popular stories and narratives—all the while doing supposedly comical reenactments of racial stereotypes.

"The minstrel tradition really starts in the United States in the 1830s," Hamill explains, "and it becomes extremely popular because it was a performance tradition for working-class audiences."

And one such minstrel theater was Ordway Hall in downtown Boston, where James Lord Pierpont's new song was performed—in blackface—for the first time in 1857. Now, again, "Jingle Bells" is not explicitly about Christmas, or any holiday at all, for that matter. It's about sleigh rides. And while nowadays, sleigh rides conjure images of nostalgic postcard Christmases, in the 19th century, sleigh rides and sleigh culture—which, yes, was very much a thing—had a different meaning.

"Omnibus sleigh-riding was a necessary part of moving about Boston in the 19th century, and also New York, in the northern climate," says Hamill. "So to move around, they would have these adapted ships, in some cases, that were turned into omnibuses. And they would basically carry people around like mass transit on sleighs."

TO
JOHN P. ORDWAY, ESQ.

The

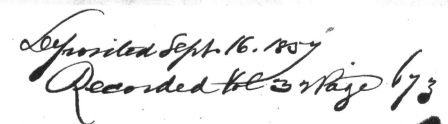

ONE HORSE OPEN SLEIGH

SONG
and
CHORUS

Written & composed by

J. PIERPONT.

BOSTON
Published by OLIVER DITSON & Co 277 Washington St

C. C. CLAPP & Co.   BECK & LAWTON.   TRUAX & BALDWIN.   S. T. GORDON.
Boston   Philadª   Cincinnati   N. York

Entered according to act of Congress A D 1857 by O. Ditson & Co in the Clerks Office of the Dist Court of Mass

"Oh what fun / It is to ride . . ."

And from that ubiquity and cultural importance came a common sleigh-ride narrative. "You can see it in the visual culture," notes Hamill, "you can see it in a lot of the songs; there's many more sleigh-ride songs other than just 'Jingle Bells.' There's kind of a conventional aspect to a lot of the sleigh-ride songs, poems, and stories. And you can even see it in the visual culture: There's a courtship ritual; there is some kind of male display; there is usually drinking involved. There is an upset, in some way, so that there's a kind of falling out of the sleigh. And then there is music involved, so one of the aspects of this layered narrative is to sing about the whole experience of going out in a sleigh."

"A sleighing song tonight"

So if sleigh-ride culture inspired so many songs, why is "Jingle Bells" the only one that's still around? There are a couple of ways to explain this. One of them has to do with the relationship between the original music publisher, Oliver Ditson, and Ordway Hall in Boston.

Hamill reveals, "Right next door to Ordway Hall is a place called Oliver Ditson and Company, which is the place that publishes the music that would have been performed in the hall. So imagine if you attended a minstrel performance, you liked the music, and then you went next door and you could purchase the sheet music. Then you could take it home, and you could play it on the piano at home."

This was at a time when more and more homes had pianos; it's still several years away from recorded music, and several more still from radio. If you heard music in your home, it was usually because someone bought the sheet music and played it on the home piano.

Secondly, in a very James Lord Pierpont move, he republished the song in 1859. And that's when the song got its now-familiar title. "The first publication is 'The One-Horse Open Sleigh,'" Hamill explains. "And then the 1859 [version] is 'Jingle Bells, or The One-Horse Open Sleigh.' And that's James Pierpont republishing it—most likely, he made a little bit more money by republishing it and just retitling it."

Which brings us back to where we started—to that plaque in Medford, Massachusetts, claiming that in 1850, Pierpont wrote the song at a local tavern. There's another side to this story, which goes a little something like this: In 1857, Pierpont was living in Savannah, Georgia, where

The Other Two Verses

When, as children, we are taught the song "Jingle Bells," we pretty much get the chorus plus the first verse. (You know, the one that starts with "Dashing through the snow . . .") But there are three verses to the song. Some recordings make their way through the whole thing—no one says "upsot" like Barbra Streisand—but many just stick to the first verse.

As "Jingle Bells" expert Kyna Hamill points out, sleighing songs often dealt with courtship and with the sleigh falling over, and you only get those if you dig deeper into the lyrics. Impress your friends, or perhaps your fellow carolers, by learning the second and third verses of this holiday favorite:

A day or two ago,
I thought I'd take a ride,
And soon Miss Fanny Bright
Was seated by my side;
The horse was lean and lank
Misfortune seemed its lot
We got into a drifted bank,
And then we got upsot.

Now the ground is white
Go it while you're young
Take the girls tonight
And sing a sleighing song.
Just get a bob-tailed bay [or, in some versions, "bob-tailed nag"]
Two-forty for its speed
Hitch him to an open sleigh
And crack! You'll take the lead.

If you really want to show off your Christmas spirit and knowledge of dead languages, wow them with a rendition of "Jingle Bells" in Latin:

Nives glacies
Nox pueritia
Risus decunt nunc
Decent carmina!
Laetos iuvat nos
Ire per agros
Traha fert velociter,
Et cachinemus nos!

O tinniat, tinniat
Tintinnabulum!
Labimur in glacie
Post mulum curtum!

Tinniat, tinniat
Tintinnabulum!
Labimur in glacie
Post mulum curtum!

he was the musical director of a Unitarian church. Some people have claimed that he wrote the song while he was living there. It convinced enough people that, in 1985, the mayor of Savannah erected a commemorative marker across the street from that church.

That didn't sit too well with the folks in Medford. So a few years later, the mayor of Medford wrote an angry letter to the mayor of Savannah, declaring Medford to have the true and rightful claim. The mayor of Savannah replied with an angry letter of his own, standing his ground. And nearly 30 years later, both places continue to claim ownership, with neither side willing to budge, without too much to go on in terms of settling the score once and for all. So we'll just have to leave things there.

CHAPTER 15

CHRISTMAS LIGHTS

We Didn't Start the Fire

Legend has it that Martin Luther was the first person to place lit candles on a Christmas tree. He was inspired, the story goes, by the image of the stars glowing brightly on the first Christmas Eve, and he wanted to re-create that effect on the Christmas tree, which was a decoration that originated in his native Germany.

As nice a story as it is, it's almost certainly not true. The earliest references to candles on Christmas trees date back to about a century after Martin Luther's time. But let's pause for a moment to consider that, at some point in history, someone thought it would be a good idea to put lit candles on a tree. Not only that, but also that the idea caught on.

Ablaze with Christmas Spirit

You could say the idea spread like wildfire, but that's just a little too close to the actual truth. Besides, having lit candles on your Christmas tree is a problem in more ways than one. In the first place, how do you attach them to the tree? Originally, people would melt a bit of candle wax onto a branch and then stick the bottom of a candlestick into the wax and let it act as a kind of adhesive.

This wasn't foolproof, of course: If you could get the candles to stay upright in the first place, the wax wouldn't always hold, and they'd fall off. So along the way people innovated—some would use a pin to pierce through the candlestick and into the branch to hold it in place. This worked OK, but it didn't stop some enterprising folks from coming up with further innovations.

In the early 1800s, someone invented long rods that attached to the tree's trunk and extended outward. At the end of the rod was a small clip for holding a candle steady. Later that century, candle holders that clipped onto the branches hit the market, but there were still major problems, like the fact that the candles dripped wax onto the tree and whatever was beneath it.

And then there was the most obvious problem of all; you had lit candles on a tree that was indoors. You couldn't keep it lit for more than a half hour at a time, and it needed constant supervision. People would even keep buckets of sand and water nearby in case of emergency. An 1896 issue of *Good Housekeeping* advised readers: "It is advisable to have a bucket of water and a sponge fastened to a stick of sufficient length to reach the top of the tree near at hand, in order to extinguish any flame which may arise."

But those precautions weren't always enough—Christmas-tree fires were so common that some insurance companies refused to cover them. But all of that was about to change in 1882 with the invention of what would forever change the face of Christmas trees (and then, eventually, houses and hedges and displays in the center of town) and make Christmas brighter and more colorful and, thankfully, safer for all of us.

Enter Edison

In order to have the electric Christmas light, you must first have electricity. Electrification of homes began in the 1880s, so it's amazing to think that the electric Christmas light was introduced in 1882. It was really among the first practical applications of electric light, and the honor of the first electrically lit Christmas tree goes to Edward Johnson, who worked for Thomas Edison's Electric Light Company.

The tree was in Johnson's New York City living room. Johnson's house was one of the few in New York City that had been wired for electricity. The light bulbs, all 80 of them, had been specially made just for him and hand-wired individually.

Johnson's Christmas lights caught people's attention, and other people wanted them, although for the first 20 years or so, they were mainly a luxury item for the very well-off. One of those well-off people was President Grover Cleveland. During his second term in 1895, he sponsored the first electrically lit Christmas tree in the White House. It had a whopping 100 lights on it, and that was a big deal at the time.

Bright, but Not Cheap

In the meantime, because old traditions die hard, and also because Christmas lights were just out of reach for most people, candles on trees continued to be a custom in a lot of households. But in 1903, General Electric offered the first pre-wired string of Christmas lights for sale. The strings held just eight lights. You can buy strings of 500 nowadays for $20 or $30, but in 1903, 8 lights cost around $12, which was just a little less than the average weekly income for many households. Despite the cost, they gradually caught on, and by the 1930s, the electric Christmas light finally replaced the candle on Christmas trees in most homes.

Once again, people were inspired to innovate. The first lights were either round or pear-shaped, but some European makers produced figural lights in the shape of Santa Claus, animals, or characters. And then in 1936, a man named Carl Otis, an accountant for the Montgomery Ward department store, came up with a new kind of Christmas light that added an effervescent glow to the Christmas tree: the bubble light. These are lights attached to glass tubes filled with a liquid chemical, and the liquid bubbles when the lights warm up.

One of the world's most famous lit Christmas tree displays appears each year in New York City's Rockefeller Center. The 2021 tree was 79 feet tall, and required 50,000 LED lights on nearly 5 miles of wire.

According to George Johnson, author of the book *Christmas Ornaments, Lights and Decorations,* "[Bubble lights] started right before World War II, in terms of an invention, but it was in the late '40s and into the '50s that they became the phenomena that they were." Although Carl Otis was the inventor, he lost the copyright to produce them—bad for him, but good for Christmas trees, because other companies would put them out and continue to innovate.

"Quite a few companies put them out," Johnson continues. "They were distinguished by the plastic base that the lamp was housed in. And also by the patterns that the bubbles made. Some of them had a very large bubble, which had a glass slug in the bottom of the tube, or a chemical crystal that helped with the bubbling—those appeared to be very popular at the time, because the bubble was very big. It was almost like a glug, glug, glug, and the large bubble went up. They were very easy to see inside the glass tubes. The rarest of the bubble lights was one called a shooting star: It had a mixture of two different types of chemicals, and essentially the bubble was shot up from the bottom to the top of the tube and then cascaded down, almost like a firework."

And the Wheel Goes 'Round

Just like their predecessors, bubble lights originally came in strings of eight or nine. And most sets still on the market today contain only about that many. As sensational as they were, trends come and go, and this one just wasn't meant to last. "By the 60s, they were gone, because people had aluminum trees with a color wheel and no lights on their tree," says Johnson. "The color wheel

Brightly decorated trees, homes, and town squares have been a facet of Christmas movies pretty much as long as there have been movies. But two comedies take Christmas lights—and the extremes to which some people will use them—as fodder for laughs.

When National Lampoon's Christmas Vacation *first hit theaters in 1989, it was established from the two previous vacation movies that suburban dad Clark Griswold (played by Chevy Chase) never does anything when he can possibly overdo it, instead. So for Clark's family Christmas, it's not enough just to put lights on his house—he's got to put all the lights on his house. (And according to some estimates, he's got about 25,000 incandescent lights festooning his home.)*

What was originally meant to be a joke about holiday excess has become, over the years, aspirational instead. In 2017, the retail chain Bed Bath & Beyond began selling the officially branded "National Lampoon's Christmas Vacation LED Light Set" (also listed as "Clark Griswold 768-Bulb LED Cluster Rice Outdoor String Lights"), promising "More Lights Per Foot!"

Less successful at the box office, but still in regular rotation around Christmastime, is the 2006 comedy Deck the Halls, *starring Danny DeVito as a brash homeowner who shakes up a community's traditional Christmas with his ostentatious plan to put up enough lights to be seen from space. No spoilers as to whether or not the character achieves his ambitious goal, but a researcher decided to quantify just how many lights would be required on one house to make it visible from Earth's orbit.*

Just in case that's a goal for your own decorating this year, the number was 2,683 LED lights on the roof—but only in an area with minimal light pollution.

itself provided the light to sparkle that the lights and the different colors of the ornaments themselves on the tree would have provided."

Christmas lights of all kinds have found their way off the Christmas tree and onto mantles, windows, and of course, the outside of homes, whether they're covered in old-school strings of large, incandescent multicolored lights, or bedecked with thousands of tiny LED bulbs. Let's remember, though, that with great Christmas spirit comes great responsibility. Some of these house displays get a little out of hand. There's even a TV show called *The Great Christmas Light Fight*, which shows just how extreme this stuff can get. Ultimately, there's nothing like a tasteful, understated light display to make the season merry and, literally, bright.

CHAPTER 16

"SILENT NIGHT"

The Christmas Carol with a Skeleton in Its Closet—Literally

Just hearing the opening notes of "Silent Night" takes you to an unmistakably Christmasy place. It's by far the best known Christmas song in the world, and probably among the most recognizable songs in any genre, which makes perfect sense when you consider that it's been recorded more times than any other song in history.

It's a study in minimalism, with a sparse melody and moderate tempo. It has a tranquil, open feel, like a lullaby. Perfect listening for any time during the season, whether or not all is calm or bright. If you're like most people, you've never known a Christmas season where "Silent Night" wasn't an essential part of the soundscape.

And that fact alone is remarkable, when you consider the song's humble beginnings, its nearly accidental debut, and its unlikely journey throughout Europe and America. That's a story involving an exhumation, singing glove makers, mice with the munchies, and a pair of friends who wouldn't let a little thing like a broken church organ make for a silent night . . . except, that they actually did.

Redeeming Grace, for 200 Years and Counting

In 1818, on Christmas Eve, in a tiny village called Oberndorf in Austria, at a chapel with the Christmasy name of St. Nicholas Church, "Silent Night" was performed for the first time. But that's not really where our story begins. Where the story truly starts is somewhat in the eye of the beholder: Perhaps it begins at the end of the Napoleonic Wars, just a few years earlier. People were recovering from the violence and grateful for peace. Maybe that's what inspired the young priest named Joseph Mohr to write a poem titled "Silent Night, Holy Night" (or "Stille Nacht, Heilige Nacht" in its original German).

Or we could start with Mohr's visit to one of the families in his flock, where seeing a sickly baby inspired him to write the poem. Or was it that he was inspired on a walk from his grandfather's home to church, years before? Or maybe it was those hungry church mice that chewed up the church organ bellows, forcing a change of plans for the Christmas Eve service's musical accompaniment? These are all common ways that the story has been told and retold over the years, but the problem is they're all half-true at best, if not entirely false.

D̶ID Y̶OU K̶NOW?

St. Nicholas Church in Oberndorf, known locally as the Stille-Nacht-Kapelle (Silent Night Chapel), hosted festivities in 2018 to celebrate the bicentennial of "Silent Night." According to tour guide Herman Schneider, the event attracted visitors from such far-flung locales as the United States, Iceland, and even Sri Lanka, with guests all singing the song in their native languages.

"A romanticized version is that a mouse got in and chewed up the bellows of the organ, but from what we know, that is not true. The organ was broken down." So says Wayne Bronner, president and CEO of Bronner's Christmas Wonderland in Frankenmuth, Michigan. It's unclear what mischievous mice are supposed to add to the story, but that certainly is one of the several little pieces of legend that has been added over the centuries.

Here's what we do know: Joseph Mohr was born to an unmarried embroiderer and a mercenary father in 1792. He had an aptitude for music, served as a singer and violinist in church choirs while growing up. Being an "illegitimate" child was a problem for him when he sought to enter the seminary in 1811, but he was able to get an exemption. After graduating in 1815, he served as priest in the town of Mariapfarr for two years. During this time, he wrote a six-stanza poem titled

The Silent Night Chapel in Oberndorf bei Salzburg, Austria. WIKIMEDIA COMMONS

"Silent Night, Holy Night." He wrote lots of poems and song lyrics, and as far as anyone can tell, he had no plans of turning it into a song or having it published. Apparently, he tucked the poem away in his collection and didn't pay any special attention to it.

In 1817, when Mohr was in his early 20s, he was assigned to the St. Nicholas Church in the town of Oberndorf in 1817. The move was to provide temporary assistance to the parish priest, and soon Mohr was assigned the role of Koadjutor (assistant priest). It was here that Mohr met Franz Gruber, a schoolteacher and musician from nearby Arnsdorf. Gruber served as St. Nicholas Church's organist and choirmaster.

Fast forward to 1818. As Christmas is approaching, Mohr is getting ready for the Christmas Eve service, including the music part. As Mohr was making last-minute preparations and double checking that everything was in order, he noticed that the church organ wouldn't play—that much is definitely true—but it was flooding from the nearby river that damaged the organ, the same flooding that would soon force the church to close altogether.

There would be no organ music that Christmas, so Mohr did some quick thinking. How about a song that didn't need an organ? He dug up his poem and went over to Gruber's house. He asked him how quickly he could set the poem to music. The most famous Christmas song in the world was a result of a mishap, some resourceful thinking, and basically a rush job on some music writing.

Silent Night, the Cartoon

If you prefer the version of the story where mischievous mice are the real culprits behind the broken organ, why not check out Silent Night, Holy Night, *the 1976 cartoon special from Hanna-Barbera? The part about the mice isn't the only liberty taken in this telling of the story. In it, Joseph Mohr is at odds with Oberndorf's Bürgermeister (the mayor, essentially), who stresses the importance of the annual Christmas concert for bringing in tourism dollars. In search of a replacement part for the organ, Franz Gruber sets out with his two young sons on a trip to Salzburg, only to encounter one dangerous obstacle after another. No spoilers here, but let's just say that when it comes to the part about writing "Silent Night," there are some additional sources of inspiration for the lyrics and melody.*

It's a sweet and largely forgotten cartoon special, though the religious theme throughout is not something found in most modern animated Christmas specials.

"They sang it that first night accompanied by a guitar, which was relatively unusual, because all the church music to that point had been on an organ," says Bronner. That part was remarkable as well. Not only was it unusual to play church music on a guitar, it was actually kind of inappropriate. In that time and place, a guitar was mostly an instrument you'd see a musician playing in a pub.

The story could have ended here—and in fact, it really should have. A last-minute fire drill for a service at a small church in a small town? There's no reason the song shouldn't have been instantly forgotten. But it spread to the neighboring towns and then farther still, and here we are today. This is where some more legends and half-truths come into the story: Some say that the church organ repairman heard the song when he came to fix the organ and he helped to spread it as he went from town to town. But something we know for sure is that traveling folk-singer groups were common in the 19th century, and many of these groups learned the song and repeated it in their travels.

The following year, Mohr moved on to his next assignment in Kuchl. As the song continued to spread, the names of its creators were forgotten. There was a decades-long period where the true authorship was unknown. It appeared in some songbooks as "author unknown" and had sometimes even been attributed to Haydn, Mozart, or Beethoven. In 1854, the Royal Prussian Court Orchestra in Berlin made an inquiry to the St. Peter's Abbey in Salzburg, assuming that Haydn was the author and asking whether St. Peter's had a copy of the music in its archive. In December of that year, Gruber responded with detailed documentation of the song's origins in a letter that is currently archived at the Silent Night Museum in Hallein, Austria.

Coming to America (and Elsewhere)

According to Bronner, "Two groups of singers—the Strassers and the Rainers—took the song throughout Europe." The Strasser family was a group of singing glove makers. (And how awesome is that?) They performed the song in front of a large audience in 1832, which was a big boost for its popularity. Bronner continues, "Eventually, the Rainer group brought it to New York City, and it's grown since that time to become the world's favorite Christmas hymn."

That was in 1839. Within a few decades, the song had been translated into more than 20 languages. In 1859 John Freeman Young, an Episcopal priest in New York City, published the English translation we're most familiar with, translating three of the original six verses. And somewhere along the line, the title was shortened from "Silent Night, Holy Night" to simply "Silent Night."

Mohr would go on to several more assignments throughout his career. He died at 55 from respiratory disease in 1848. Throughout his life, Mohr never had a portrait done of him, which created a little problem in 1912 when a sculptor wanted to create a memorial of Mohr and Gruber. So, the sculptor had Mohr's body exhumed, and he removed his skull from the grave to use as an artist's model for the statue. The skull was kept in storage for years, but when a memorial chapel was erected at the site where the St. Nicholas Church once stood, the skull was embedded in the wall of the chapel, and it's still there today. You can visit it, just as tens of thousands of people do each year. Or you could go to Frankenmuth, Michigan, where Wayne Bronner's family has constructed a scale replica.

CHAPTER 17

GIFT WRAP

How French Envelope-Liners Changed Christmas Forever

Those stories about famous products that were invented by accident are always fascinating. Maybe you've heard the one about the naval engineer who was working with tension springs, and when he dropped one on the floor, he noticed that it almost looked like it was crawling. And the next thing you know, the Slinky is one of the top-selling toys on the market. Or how about the one about the company that was trying to make a super-strong adhesive, but when they failed, they sold the result anyway, as Post-It notes?

Here's one that maybe you haven't heard. It's about two brothers who ran a stationery store in Kansas City. The year was 1917, and like most retailers at the time, they offered customers plain tissue paper to use as wrapping paper. Only, back then it wasn't known as "giftwrap" or "wrapping paper." It was referred to as "gift dressings."

One day, during the Christmas season, the store ran out of gift dressings. So Raleigh, one of the brothers, went back to the warehouse to look for something else, anything they could use as a substitute. He found a stack of fancy, brightly colored paper sheets imported from France that they had planned on using as the inner linings of their envelopes. He brought some of it back to the store, priced the sheets at 10 cents a pop, and the stuff just flew off the shelves. They couldn't keep up with demand.

And just like that, a whole new industry was born. The wrapping paper we know and love today, with its bright colors and printed patterns, can trace its beginnings back to that one day, and that one decision, made in 1917 by a man named Rollie Hall. Along with his brother J. C., Rollie ran a company that's still around today. Maybe you've heard of it: Hallmark.

When Gifts Stopped Being Naked

What's even more interesting is the fact that, when all of this happened, the idea of wrapping gifts for Christmas was only about 50 years old. It seems unimaginable that there was ever a time when gifts wouldn't be wrapped. Think of the anticipation created by the concealment of gift wrap, or the beauty of a decoratively wrapped gift, the excitement of unwrapping to reveal the surprise of what's inside. All of that is relatively new. And there's an interesting story behind it, one that has to do with the influence of media, the rise of industrialization, and the birth of consumer culture.

Let's go back to sometime a little before 1850. Back then, Christmas still wasn't a major shopping or gift-giving holiday. What few gifts were given were mostly for children (and, for the wealthy, servants). They were almost never wrapped, and were mainly small items, left in a stocking hung by the chimney, or simply handed over to the recipient.

But around this time, a new trend was starting to take hold in America that would change the face of Christmas, and profoundly influence Christmas gift giving: the Christmas tree. This was still a very new idea to most Americans, though some German settlers in Pennsylvania had brought the tradition with them. But the Christmas tree had recently gotten a helping hand from the print media. Two years earlier, in 1848, the *London Illustrated News* printed a special supplement that included a woodcut engraving of Queen Victoria, Prince Albert, and their children gathered around a table-top tree decorated with sweets and ornaments, lit with candles. The following Christmas, the Christmas tree had become a major trend in England. In 1850, *Godey's Lady's Book*, a popular women's magazine, published a version of the Victoria and Albert image.

As the Christmas tree caught on, it became common to place those small Christmas gifts on the tree, either hung from, or wedged between, the tree's branches.

All of this coincided with a time of increasing industrialization, where more goods were being produced in large factories and shipped long distances. These products needed to be protected during shipping and to be neatly stored in warehouses and on store shelves. As a result, product packaging became more common. And many of these packaged items were too big to go in the tree. Not

This influential image of Victoria and Albert in front of a Christmas tree with their family appeared in Godey's Lady's Book in 1850. The image was altered from the original, published in The London Illustrated News in 1848. In this version, Albert's sash and moustache have been removed, as has Victoria's tiara. WIKIMEDIA COMMONS

Did You Know?

*The trend toward products sold in boxes
inspired new lines of products that could
only be sold in boxes: things like board
games and jigsaw puzzles. These, in turn,
became popular Christmas gifts.*

only that, but by the late 19th century, adults were giving each other Christmas gifts on a routine basis. That's a lot of gifts, suddenly, many of them large, and not enough tree space to hold them. An 1896 issue of *Good Housekeeping* specifically advised: "It would be pretty to arrange the gifts about the base of the tree instead of hanging them upon the tree as is customary amongst Americans."

Around this time, wrapping gifts for adults and children alike really took hold. Wrapped boxes were covered in tissue paper, usually plain white, but Sears and other stores sold colored tissue paper. At this point in the timeline, we're still 20 years away from when the Hall brothers would offer their brightly colored luxury paper as gift wrap, but in the decades leading up to that moment, wrapping gifts in tissue had become not only the norm but also a booming business. And the captain of that industry was the Dennison Manufacturing Company.

Dennison made a name for itself by inventing the white adhesive rings that commonly go around holes punched in paper to keep it from tearing. These were created back in the Civil War days as a way to keep shipping tags from falling off of packages. Dennison would go on to produce all kinds of paper products, including adhesive Christmas seals and plain-white-tissue gift dressings.

Maybe the real genius of Dennison was their flair for marketing. They'd offer live workshops in their stores on how to wrap gifts, and also in department stores where their products were sold.

The Holly and the . . . Holly

"People would take Denison's Christmas seals, use the tissue paper, and then they put the seals all over the packages and make their own designs." That's according to Pat Lavin, author of Welcome to Dennison Manufacturing Co., *a history of that company. She's also a volunteer at the Framingham History Center in Framingham, Massachusetts. That's where Dennison's factory operated for almost a century. In 1908, Dennison first advertised tissue paper with a simple holly design printed on it.*

"Interestingly enough, for 15 to 20 years, people were perfectly happy with this one holly design between 1910 and 1925. They [later] came up with all these other patterns, because people then wanted the various designs, but it took a long time for them to really ask for [something different]."

Hallmark & Christmas—They Cared Enough

The Hall brothers' discovery of gift wrap was just one step on a long journey that paired Hallmark and Christmas. In addition to the company's many cards and gift wrap selections for the holiday, the company created Hallmark Keepsake Ornaments in the 1970s. It's a line of Christmas tree decorations that has grown so popular that the company now has a Keepsake Ornaments membership organization, where people pay an annual fee to be among the first to see the catalog of each year's releases (and to purchase them, of course).

And while fans who tune in every year for all the Christmas movies on Hallmark Channel and Hallmark Movies & Mysteries might think the company's history of TV entertainment reaches back to November 30, 2002—that's when the very first Hallmark Channel Christmas movie, Santa, Jr., *debuted—it's a legacy that stretches all the way back to the very beginning of the medium. Hallmark took a gamble on the then-new phenomenon of television in 1951 with the institution of* Hallmark Television Playhouse, *a continuation of the popular radio program* Hallmark Playhouse.*

Hallmark Television Playhouse *would eventually evolve into* Hallmark Hall of Fame, *one of the longest-running and most-awarded series in TV history, and the very first* Hallmark Television Playhouse *also just happened to be a Christmas presentation: the world premiere of* Amahl and the Night Visitors, *the very first opera ever composed for television, which aired live from Studio 8H at Rockefeller Center on December 24, 1951. Gian Carlo Menotti's opera tells the story of young Amahl and his mother, who receive a visit from the Three Wise Men who are following the Star of Bethlehem.*

In recent years, Hallmark's involvement with Christmas includes the written word—Hallmark Publishing, established in 2017, kicked off with a novelization of the highly rated Hallmark Channel movie Journey Back to Christmas, *and the company's year-round slate of novels always includes several Christmas titles, some adapted from Hallmark Channel movies and others that have become the source material for future films.*

More than 100 years after Raleigh Hall grabbed that festive paper from the warehouse, Hallmark remains very much in the Christmas business.

This was something no one else was doing at the time. They even had their own radio show dedicated to the subject.

Whatever Dennison and others did to turn people on to wrapping paper, it obviously worked. Nowadays, we spend over $2 billion a year on the stuff, and one company alone—American Greetings—sold more than 1.7 billion linear feet of wrapping paper in a single year. That's enough to circle the planet 12 times. There was even a series of psychological experiments published in the 90s that found that we like gifts better when they're wrapped. Not only that, but the nicer the wrapping, the more we like the gift.

CHAPTER 18

SNOW GLOBES

The Little Medical Device That Couldn't

Imagine an old-fashioned operating theater—and "theater" is the appropriate word, because as a patient lay on the table surrounded by doctors and nurses and medical equipment, tiers of amphitheater-style seating would surround the scene, with rows and rows of medical students watching and learning. It's around 1850. No one's wearing masks or gloves. There's no sterilization of environment or equipment. Wide acceptance of the "germ theory of disease" was still a few years away. So a surgical room packed with onlookers was perfectly normal at the time.

Nurse, I Can't See in Here

And if that sounds antiquated, wait 'til you hear about the lighting: Operating rooms in those days were built facing the southeast, with windows in the ceilings to make use of sunlight. Edison's light bulbs were still 30 or so years into the future. Operations could only happen at certain times of day, and only if it wasn't overcast. Not only that, but it was all too easy for the surgeons to block their own light while they were working.

Let's pause for a moment and be grateful that we all live in the 21st century. There were some attempts to use mirrors to reflect light, but they were unreliable and, besides, they created a lot of heat. Some rooms were lit by gas lamps which, again, generated excessive heat and made the air dirty. And even when electric light bulbs did come on the market, those early ones weren't powerful enough to meet the needs of an operating room.

So, the next thing you know, we had—snow globes? There are a few more details involved in connecting those dots, yes, but those are indeed points A and B of our story. In between, there are shoemakers, World War II, Austrian souvenir shops, baby food, and a super-top-secret process for creating fake snow—one that literally only one person on earth knows. (More on him in a moment.)

The snow globe is one of those items that seems like it could have been around forever. No windup clockwork, no batteries; just a simple scene like a house or a famous building encased in a water-filled globe and mounted on a pedestal. You shake it up, and glittering snow whirls around the scene as it slowly falls. But snow globes are a relatively new invention, and it wasn't until decades after their invention that they'd become more or less exclusively a Christmas decoration.

A Failure Becomes a Success

To start our story, we need to go to Vienna, Austria, and meet a man named Erwin Perzy III. "My grandfather, Erwin Perzy, his business was surgical instruments," Perzy explains, "and his customers, the surgeons, asked my grandfather to improve Edison's light bulb. Edison's electric light bulb would be the perfect light, but it was not bright enough."

So his first idea was to augment Edison's light bulb by putting a glass lens in front of it. The problem was a) the glass lens was too big and expensive to make it a viable product, and b) it didn't work that great anyway, so he kept looking around for inspiration.

Perzy continues, "And so my grandfather saw, at the shoemaker's workbench, a glass globe filled with water. And behind this glass globe, the shoemaker burned a candle; the light of the candle [was] magnified by this water-filled glass globe. My grandfather grabbed this idea, and he used a water-filled glass globe instead of the solid glass lens, and he received just a small light spot. My grandfather was not very happy with this."

But he thought he might be onto something. Maybe there was something he could do with the water to amplify the light. So he got the idea of crushing up glass into a fine glitter, creating thousands and thousands of tiny reflectors—but the glass was much heavier than the water, and it sank to the bottom quickly. One day inspiration struck in the unlikeliest of places: the cupboard.

"He found a white powder in the kitchen of his mother," notes Perzy. "Semolina, used for baby food. He poured this powder into this water-filled glass globe, and when he looked in the globe, it looked like snowfall, because these little flakes floated very slowly to the ground."

The semolina did stay afloat a little better, but it still wasn't quite the perfect solution—the perfect solution for lighting an operating room, anyway—but it was perfect for a friend of Perzy's.

"A friend of my grandfather, he operated a little souvenir shop next to a church here in Austria," says Perzy. "It's a favorite pilgrim site, and this friend sold candles and Christmas crosses and all these things. He asked my grandfather to make a little miniature of the basilica—my grandfather made this little church on his workbench, and he mounted the church in the water-filled glass globe, filled with semolina. And he gave this glass globe to his friend, [who] sold it right away."

And that's the story about how in 1900 in Vienna, Austria, a surgical device–maker unintentionally created that iconic symbol of Christmas recognized the world over. Or at least, it's the beginning of the story. Perzy never did find his perfect solution for operating rooms, so he eventually abandoned the project. But seeing the potential of this new thing he created, he spent the next five years working up a system for mass-producing the items for sale in souvenir shops.

Two World Wars Later . . .

To get to where we are now, we're going to have to move one generation and one Erwin Perzy forward in time. So now we're in the years just after World War II; the country is occupied by foreign troops, and Erwin Perzy, Jr. worked part-time at the *Vienna Courier*, a newspaper run by American troops.

According to Perzy, "My father was working for these people, and they saw the snow globes, and they said, 'This would be a wonderful product for the United States, if there [were] no church inside.' My father's idea was changing the pilgrim souvenir to a Christmas item, and [he] made a Christmas tree [with] Santa Claus and a snowman."

The Subgenre of Snow Globe Cinema

Snow globes aren't just tchotchkes—in the world of made-for-TV Christmas movies, they're a trope. Whether they have magical powers or offer portals to parallel universes, snow globes make a splash on the small screen every December. Here are some favorites:

- Snowglobe *(2007):* Christina Milian stars as a Christmas-loving New Yorker who receives the titular item from an anonymous benefactor; when she falls asleep, she emerges in the picture-perfect world inside the globe. Complications arise when the residents of that world follow her to Manhattan.
- A Snow Globe Christmas *(2013):* A stressed-out director of made-for-TV Christmas movies (played by Alicia Witt) bonks her head and wakes up inside the idyllic world of her snow globe—where she's married to her long-estranged college sweetheart (Donald Faison). Just to complicate matters, this one also *features Christina Milian, as a woman who might be one of Santa's helpers.*
- Christmas in Evergreen *(2017):* The local diner in the holiday-obsessed town of Evergreen, Vermont, boasts a magical, wish-granting snow globe,

Ashley Williams with the magic snow globe from The Hallmark Channel's Christmas in Evergreen *movies.* PHOTOFEST

one that proves its powers again and again over the course of four (and counting) chapters. The snow globe becomes a major plot component (It breaks! There's a secret inside! They repair the globe!) in the third entry, Christmas in Evergreen: Tidings of Joy *(2019).*
- Kitchen Christmas Wish *(2017): OK, this one's not real—it's part of a* Saturday Night Live *parody about Hallmark Christmas movies—but the premise of a woman stuck inside of a snow globe had become so established as a plot for these movies that it was ripe for satire on SNL.*

It wasn't until about 1950 when the snow globe came to America (and got a secular overhaul) that it became a Christmas tradition. And while many companies manufacture them nowadays, the Perzy family factory has been in continuous operation ever since those early days.

Still a Secret, Passed from Generation to Generation

Today, Erwin Perzy III runs the show. Although by the time you read this, he will have stepped down—from management, anyway. "I represent the third generation working on snow globes," reveals Perzy. "And my daughter, she is the fourth generation, and she will be taking over in a couple months. But I will retire on paper, you know, because making snow globes is my life, and I love my job."

Before he retires—on paper or otherwise—he'll have to pass on a family secret: That process for making the snow is closely guarded. Erwin Jr. wouldn't share the secret with Erwin III until after he earned his master's degree.

"And I played the same thing with my daughter now," Perzy admits. "It's a very special process to create the snow, and there are some tricks you need to use. This is my personal secret. The day when she takes over, I will tell her."

Until they have that conversation, Erwin III is the only person in the world who currently knows the secret. "I have a special machine for the production of the snow, and this machine is not in my factory. It's in my private house."

CHAPTER 19

POINSETTIAS

Mexican Folklore Meets American Ingenuity

Once upon a time, there was a young girl in Mexico named Pepita. And as Christmas arrived, Pepita visited her village church for Christmas services and to leave an offering at the church's nativity scene. The only problem was that she had no offering to offer. She couldn't show up empty-handed, not for an occasion like this. So the best that little Pepita could do was gather whatever weeds she could pull up from the roadside and form them into a crude and rather shabby bouquet. Pepita felt ashamed that she had nothing better to offer. But according to the legend, she went up toward the nativity scene, knelt down to leave her bouquet of weeds, and as she did, those weeds miraculously transformed into bright red flowers, with large pointy petals growing in a shape that vaguely suggested a star.

They were the same flowers that had long been prized as much for their beauty as for their use as medicine and pigmentation. They were once widely employed for their sticky white sap known as latex, which was believed to treat fevers and headaches. Others used the leaves to make red or purple dye. And that flower (which had been known by many names), because of that legend, would go on to be known as la flor de Nochebuena, the flower of Christmas Eve.

Franciscan monks in a Mexican town had begun using these flowers in their nativity processions. And for generations, the legend of Pepita and her humble offering of a bouquet of weeds was part of the Christmas celebration for many communities in Mexico. It could have remained a regional tradition, based on a regional legend and a regional flower. But of course, it didn't stay there.

Those bright red flowers with the pointy leaves are, of course, that ubiquitous flower we now know as a poinsettia. And the story about how it came to America, how it got its name change, and how it came to be as much a part of the Christmas foliage as mistletoe and holly has some strange twists and turns to it, ones that involve a kidnapping, possibly a murder, international diplomacy, and a good old-fashioned American success story.

This tale begins in 1826 and involves that fraternal organization known as the Freemasons. "There was a man by the name of William Morgan who, in 1826, was kicked out of his Masonic Lodge," says Mark Schmeller, associate professor of history at Syracuse University. "And he threatened to write a book revealing their secret rituals and oaths. He was kidnapped and probably murdered by a group of Freemasons here in Upstate New York.

"They tried to bring the kidnappers to justice, but failed to—in many cases, the trials that they held, the juries were stacked with Freemasons who let their brothers off. It evolved into a social movement and eventually a political party that briefly existed in the late 1820s, known as the Anti-Masonic party."

Put a pin in this part—it's the prologue to the story.

Meet Mr. Poinsett

Around the same time that all of this was happening, a man by the name of Joel Roberts Poinsett was named America's ambassador to Mexico by President John Quincy Adams. "Poinsett is a learned, well-traveled, slave-owning South Carolinian, and he was involved in Democratic politics," Schmeller continues. "He goes to Mexico, with a set of instructions to promote the American system of republican government."

Poinsett had a long career and a broad education before all of this; his résumé reads like that of someone who grew up in a wealthy and privileged family in the 19th century. He studied law. He's referred to as a physician and a diplomat. He was an amateur botanist and spoke several languages. He had traveled to Europe and Russia, and he was appointed by President Madison as a Consul in General, for which he served as an agent in Chile and Argentina. In 1820, he was elected to the US House of Representatives, and later on, he was Martin Van Buren's secretary of war, a cabinet position now called secretary of defense.

Poinsett was also a Freemason, so on his mission to Mexico, he started to set up Masonic lodges there. This was nothing new—Mexico already had Masonic lodges, but those followed what Freemasons know as the Scottish Rite, while Poinsett's lodges followed what's known as York Rite.

"So he establishes these Masonic lodges, and they begin to attract Mexicans who have more pro-American points of view, who have more liberal political points of view," notes Schmeller. "And this eventually evolves into a political party in Mexico known as the Yorkinos." This new, more liberally minded political party didn't sit too well with the Mexican government. Schmeller continues, "As the Yorkinos are gaining strength, the government—which is affiliated with the Scottish Rite Masonic lodges—essentially tries to outlaw secret societies. Specifically, they want to get rid of York Rite lodges and the Yorkinos."

Not only that, but Poinsett himself became a target and also a sort of unfortunate poster boy for foreign politicians meddling in domestic affairs. "They start saying that Poinsett is behind all of this, that Yorkino lodges are really just Yankee lodges, and this gets him embroiled in a lot of controversy," says Schmeller.

"He's attacked in the newspapers and in pamphlets; as he started to defend himself, Mexicans began to use the term 'Poinsettismo,' meaning, "officious Yankee meddling." It becomes a popular term, and he becomes identified as the face of Yankee arrogance, Yankee meddling in

Mexican domestic politics. There's some irony to this, in that Poinsett had a very positive attitude towards Mexico. He wrote a very generous book about Mexico; he was considered to be the leading American authority on Mexico, but he becomes reviled in Mexico."

Coming to America

Luckily for Poinsett, and for us, there would be something else named after him. And that takes us back to the legend of Pepita and her bouquet of weeds that miraculously transformed into those bright red flowers. By Poinsett's time, these were being used in nativity displays. As Schmeller points out, "He's very impressed by this, and he sends it back to South Carolina. This catches on; it becomes very popular at flower shows."

And then, in 1836, a Scottish botanist named Robert Graham labeled the flower a "poinsettia," and the name stuck. Had it not been for Poinsett's mission to Mexico, and his interest in botany, the poinsettia may never have enjoyed the wide popularity at Christmas it does today.

That ubiquity we see nowadays—with poinsettias available at every nursery, every flower shop, every grocery store, and even in many drugstores, gas stations, and elsewhere—could only be possible with cultivation on a massive scale. And for that, we can thank a botanist named Paul Ecke. In the early 20th century, he started his poinsettia empire in southern California, at one point producing 90% of all the world's poinsettias.

Did You Know?

You don't have to worry about their safety, as many people once did. Claims that the plant is toxic to humans are still floating around, but they were disproven long ago. They're perfectly safe to have around the house.

Building a Better Flower

One of his early innovations was to sell the poinsettia as a potted plant, rather than as a floral bouquet, as they had normally been sold up till then; they didn't ship well or last long that way. Additionally, he licensed technology that allowed him to graft different poinsettia plants together to create a perfect breed for appearance and endurance. Ecke's operation is still in existence today, though the family sold the company in 2012.

Today, poinsettias account for nearly a quarter of all potted plants sold in America. And unlike mistletoe and holly and Christmas trees, which are often discarded right after Christmas, poinsettias can be maintained long term, making them a perfect way to keep the Christmas spirit alive all throughout the year.

How to Keep Your Poinsettia Alive

When the calendar rolls over to January, you can still keep those pretty poinsettias thriving and healthy in your home. Just follow these simple tips:

- Even though we associate the poinsettia with Christmas time, the plant is no fan of winter weather. Make sure you keep in a warm place, ideally between 70 and 75 degrees Fahrenheit during the day, and no cooler than 60 degrees at night—with bright (but indirect) light.
- Let the soil get dry between waterings, so the roots aren't standing in water. If the pot came with a foil wrapping, punch some holes in the bottom to enable drainage. As the leaves begin to fade, cut back the plant and allow it a rest period where it can be cooler and drier, and exposed to less light.
- When spring arrives, place it in direct light and resume regular watering (and perhaps even some fertilization).
- During the summer, morning sunlight is best. For a bushier plant, keep pinching back the growth until about mid-August.

CHAPTER 20

HOLLY

Of All the Trees That Are in the Wood, It Bears the Crown

It's no accident that traditional Christmas colors are red and green, and you don't have to look any farther than the bough decking the hall or the wreath hanging on the door to understand why evergreen plants like mistletoe and holly have been part of the Christmas tradition since the very beginning.

Maybe it's not the first thing you think of when Christmas comes to mind. It plays more of a supporting role—taking a backseat to the Christmas tree and Santa Claus and lights and snowmen and candy canes—but keep your eyes peeled for the subtle ways it helps to form the backdrop for the season. You'll find images of it on Christmas cards, holly patterns on gift wrap, and forming a bed of greens to festively display decorations and centerpieces on mantles and tabletops. And even though holly is inseparable from Christmas today, its use in traditions dates back much further than Christmas itself.

Ageless and Evergreen

Imagine you're in Northern Europe during ancient times: You're walking through a forest at winter time. The landscape is bleak. Snow blankets the ground and clings to the bare branches of trees

A Joyous
For you and those
whom you hold dear
I wish a Christmas
full of cheer.

that shed their leaves months ago. But not all forms of plant life have gone dormant—through the blanket of snow peeks out the shiny, prickly green leaves and red berries of the holly shrub. Our ancient friends believed that any plant that could thrive year-round must have something special about it.

"Holly was considered to be good luck, and it was brought into the house," says Sue Hunter, the president of the Holly Society of America, which has been promoting and sharing knowledge about holly since 1947. "When the rest of the woods went dormant during the winter time, it was a sign of hope that the world would turn green again, and it always did."

All evergreens carried that same kind of mystique, but the ones with berries got extra attention. In fact, some people believed that holly had supernatural powers, including the ability to help people see into the future. One ritual called for picking leaves off a sprig of holly and tying them up inside a handkerchief and then placing them under a pillow. Sleeping on this pillow was believed to make the sleeper dream of his or her future spouse. It was also used to ward off witches and demons, and druid people would wear it in their hair for that very purpose. It was also believed to prevent lightning strikes, defend against the evil eye, and even cure diseases like rheumatism and asthma.

Oak King vs. Holly King—The Annual Battle

"In Celtic lore and mythology, after the summer solstice," notes Hunter, "that was the time the Holly King would come to rule the world and be evergreen during the shorter days and the colder days of the coming winter." In Celtic mythology, the Oak King and the Holly King were twins, fighting an endless battle for supremacy. Oak trees were considered sacred to the Celts, and they're also deciduous, meaning that their leaves come off. As winter came, the Celts marveled at how the holly, which had been hidden among the leafy oaks all year, now stood out on the bare landscape. The Holly King had won the battle, while the Oak King stood naked in defeat—until the winter solstice, after which the tides would turn, and the Oak King would reclaim the upper hand by midsummer.

Did You Know?

Holly is the subject of an unusual—and thankfully, antiquated—Welsh tradition. It was once the custom that the last person to wake up on Christmas morning would receive a thrashing with a branch of holly. And, the day after Christmas (aka St. Stephen's Day or Boxing Day), the young men of the town would take to the streets to give the same treatment to any young woman they came across. The tradition was known as "holming" or "holly thrashing."

Superstition and mythology aside, the stuff just looks pretty, especially during the relatively colorless winter months, so it was used to decorate homes during the time of the winter solstice. Ancient Romans would send boughs of holly to friends during their solstice celebration of Saturnalia, because holly was used to honor Saturn, the god of agriculture during that time. They'd also use it in processions and deck images of Saturn with it.

The winter solstice celebrations in Europe laid the groundwork for Christmas celebrations that would follow, and many of the traditions from those solstice celebrations carried over, so it's no surprise that holly became part of Christmas.

Early on, it was given a religious significance. The thorns of the holly were associated with the crown of thorns, the white blossom with purity, and the red berries with blood. This relationship appears in the lyrics of the traditional British Christmas carol, "The Holly and the Ivy":

The holly bears a blossom,
As white as lily flow'r,
And Mary bore sweet Jesus Christ,
To be our dear Saviour

[. . .]

The holly bears a berry,
As red as any blood,
And Mary bore sweet Jesus Christ,
To do poor sinners good

[. . .]

The holly bears a prickle,
As sharp as any thorn,
And Mary bore sweet Jesus Christ,
On Christmas Day in the morn

According to Hunter, "Any holly brought into the house prior to Christmas Eve was considered unlucky. It was also considered a good practice to get all of the holly out of the house 12 days after Christmas and burn it to ward off evil spirits." It was believed that tossing a sprig on the Christmas fire would bring good luck.

There are about 400 species of holly. It's the English holly that we most associate with Christmas. We grow plenty of it here in the Western United States, mainly for decorative use. Even in places like California that don't succumb to a long cold winter, holly is a festive and attractive way to decorate the season.

Another Holly That Comes from England

When we think about British Christmas movies, the first ones that come to mind are various adaptations of A Christmas Carol that have been produced over the decades. But another British holiday import that is beginning to take a foothold in the United States is the drama The Holly and the Ivy (1952), which has—thanks to an increased presence on cable TV and a recent Blu-ray release—started to become a Christmastime staple on this side of the Atlantic.

Based on the play by Wynyard Browne, the film tells the story of the Gregory family in Norfolk and their annual Christmas gathering. It's an uneasy family reunion—Jenny (Celia Johnson) has been taking care of her father, village parson Martin (Ralph Richardson), but she wants to get married and leave town, knowing that she can only do so if someone else from the family steps up to be Martin's new caretaker. Martin's embittered son Michael (Denholm Elliott) chafes at Martin's plans for his life after he leaves military service, and the chic Margaret (Margaret Leighton) breezes in from her fashionable life in London, seemingly disinterested in a return to country life. But Martin's guidance and the magic of the season work together to mend the various relationships between members of the Gregory family, just in time for the church choir to perform an achingly beautiful version of the title song.

The Holly and the Ivy is a serious and dramatic film, but those looking to expand their repertoire of Christmas movies may well enjoy the graceful performances and the subtle power of its portrayal of the disappointments and, ultimately, the joys of family life.

CHAPTER 21

MISTLETOE

How Birds Spread Christmas Cheer

According to Norse myth, Baldur, son of Odin and Frigg, was a god of truth and light. One day, Baldur began having disturbing visions of his own tragic death, so Frigg set out to command every plant, every animal, and every inanimate object in the universe to swear an oath never to harm Baldur. The plan appeared to work—so well, in fact, that the other gods would make a game of it during a celebration that was held in honor of Baldur's new invincibility. If nothing in the universe could kill Baldur, then you could throw literally anything in his way, and he'd walk away unscathed. And so they did.

The game caught the attention of Loki, a god known for playing tricks and generally upsetting the status quo. He was able to find out that Frigg had actually neglected to ask one thing to swear an oath of no harm to Baldur: It was the small and harmless plant that usually was found growing off of other trees, with tapered oblong leaves and small white berries. Frigg had assumed that it was harmless to begin with, and so there was no need to solicit an oath. Loki went to the forest, found some of the plant, tore off a branch, and then returned to the party. And there he tricked Baldur's brother into throwing the branch at Baldur. The branch pierced Baldur's heart, and he died. And that plant was mistletoe.

Why would mistletoe play such an important role in a story like that? And how do we get from an ancient myth about killing a god to a modern custom of kissing beneath it at Christmas time? It's a story of superstitious ancestors, fertility rituals, the Protestant Reformation, and birds doing their business.

Plant of the Gods

The story begins way back in indeterminate ancient times, where our ancestors noticed a couple of interesting things about mistletoe: In the first place, it stayed green all year round, which was interesting enough in itself. Many ancient cultures considered most evergreens (including holly—see Chapter 20) to be somehow special. After all, why were they able to stay vibrant in the dead of winter when their woodland companions went dormant?

For that reason, they were often thought to have medicinal properties, and to have the power to bring good luck or to prevent bad luck. It was common to decorate the home with evergreen foliage like holly and mistletoe during wintertime celebrations, usually for superstitious reasons like warding off evil, or ensuring a bountiful crop for the next year.

The second thing those ancestors noticed about mistletoe is that it's always found growing high up out of another tree—a tree that would lose its leaves. No other plant did that. How was it possible? There must be something extra-special about this plant in particular, they reasoned, and legends existed that the gods dropped mistletoe onto the trees from on high. And so, because of its perceived vitality, it became associated with fertility. If only our ancestors knew the real scoop.

Kiss under the Parasite

"Mistletoe is a parasitic plant, which grows on host trees, and the plant lodges into other trees and photosynthesizes, but takes its nutrients from the tree." So says Mark Adams, whose family owns the Kiss-Me Mistletoe Farm in England. Mistletoe relies on animals to propagate; birds and some other animals would get the sticky berries—which are also the seeds—onto them somehow, and then try to rub them off on other trees. Or a bird could excrete some of the indigestible berries onto a tree, and the bird droppings helped to launch the seeds onto the tree surface.

In fact, the word "mistletoe" that we use today is derived from an earlier word in Old English that translates to something like "droppings twig." Apparently, sometime in the Middle Ages when old English was spoken, someone figured out that it wasn't the gods throwing the plant from on high, but rather the birds doing something a little more . . . earthly.

Nonetheless, the myths and legends and customs and associations persisted. It was still used medicinally—it still is, actually or at least as an alternative medicine—and it was still used as part of rituals and customs and wintertime celebrations, of which Christmas eventually became one. We do know, according to historian Gerry Bowler (author of *The World Encyclopedia of Christmas*), that some medieval English homes hung an effigy of Jesus, Mary, and Joseph, the Holy Family, inside of a wooden hoop decorated with winter greenery, under which it was customary to exchange an embrace or kiss.

After the Protestant Reformation, that image of the Holy Family disappeared, but the "kissing bunch" or "kissing bough" as it was known—a collection of greenery that often included mistletoe—remained as a Christmas custom. As a matter of fact, before the Christmas tree became the main evergreen foliage on display in the home at Christmas (which wasn't really all that long ago), it was mistletoe and holly that took that starring role.

Kiss Me Like a Pagan

And that didn't sit too well with some people, who saw mistletoe as a symbol from pre-Christian times. "It was actually seen as quite a dirty plant, by [certain segments of] Christianity," notes Adams, "so its connection with Christmas has not been that clear-cut. And in a lot of churches in the UK, [mistletoe is] still banned. It's seen as a pagan plant; pagans were not seen in the best light in the UK in the few thousand years after."

It's also likely that up until the 19th century, that custom of the kissing bough was something you'd see only among the so-called servant class. But eventually it became more widely accepted, along with the English custom of how the kissing worked. "The British tradition is every time you have a kiss, you should take a berry off," explains Adams. "So the more berries you have, the more kissing is going to happen."

When all the berries are gone, the mistletoe no longer has the power to compel people to kiss underneath it, though it does serve another use. According to Adams, "A common practice in the United Kingdom regarding what you do with the mistletoe after is that you keep it for the rest of the year, and then only replenish it the next year. That's supposed to ward off evil spirits in the pagan tradition, so you keep it up all year so it dies and shrivels up."

THE SATURDAY EVENING POST

An Illustrated Weekly Bulletin
Founded A° D! 1728

DECEMBER 14, 1912   5c. THE COPY

MORE THAN 1,900,000 CIRCULATION WEEKLY

Oh, By Gosh, By Golly, It's Time for "Mistletoe and Holly"

Mistletoe and holly are both evergreens and so, apparently, is "Mistletoe and Holly," which originally appeared on the 1957 album A Jolly Christmas with Frank Sinatra.

The song didn't become an instant classic; it never charted, and it's been covered only a handful of times. But it's a catchy number with lyrics that underscore universal holiday experiences, like "Over-eating / Merry greetings / From relatives you don't know."

"Mistletoe and Holly" has had something of a 21st century resurgence, though. It's the song Sinatra performs at the top of the 1957 Christmas episode of The Frank Sinatra Show, *and that episode was released on DVD in 2003 as* Happy Holidays with Bing and Frank *after Tina Sinatra found a 35mm color version in a family vault. (Previous home-video releases had been in black-and-white.)* Happy Holidays *offers a delightful hour of holiday music performed by Sinatra and his pal Bing Crosby, and makes a wonderful addition to the holiday season.*

The song has also gotten a new lease on life by the satellite service SiriusXM Radio—the company's year-round "Holiday Traditions" channel, which focuses on mid-20th-century Christmas music, often uses the distinctive pizzicato pluckings from the beginning of "Mistletoe and Holly" as part of the station ID breaks played between songs. (The entire tune also periodically pops up on the station.)

Granted, while "Mistletoe and Holly" has finally come into its own, it will probably forever live in the shadow of the single's flip side—Sinatra's swoony version of "The Christmas Waltz"—but it's nice to know that, like It's a Wonderful Life *(see Chapter 12) before it, an ignored piece of Christmas media can one day find its fans.*

PHOTOFEST

Of course, our American tradition is just a continuation of that English tradition, which isn't the only game in town. Adams continues, "All the European countries have slightly different twists on how they do it. I know in Italy, the tradition is to hang the mistletoe up for New Year's Eve rather than for Christmas. And in Germany, they do it for the first of Advent, so they're hanging up all their Christmas decorations a lot earlier—at the end of November, start of December."

So if the Christmas season has you feeling festively romantic, Adams some pretty simple advice: "Just hang up more mistletoe; that's the best way."

In 1893, the Oklahoma territorial legislature passed a bill declaring mistletoe its official floral emblem. Oklahoma was the last state to recognize Christmas as a holiday when it joined the Union in 1907.

CHAPTER 22

"THE TWELVE DAYS OF CHRISTMAS"

Happy Holidays, and Thanks for All the Birds

On the first day of Christmas, my true love gave to me a partridge in a pear tree. And I said, "Well, thank you, my true love. But you know, a partridge is the kind of bird that makes its nest on the ground; you wouldn't be likely to find one in a pear tree, or any other kind of tree for that matter." And my true love said to me, "Well, I didn't ask any questions. I thought of you when I saw it. I hope you like it."

And on the second day of Christmas, my true love gave to me two turtle doves and a partridge in a pear tree. And I said, "Oh, good. More birds. Tell me, why are they called "turtle" doves? And I couldn't help noticing that you're giving me a duplicate of the partridge you gave me yesterday? What's going on there?" And my true love said to me, "Look, if you don't like these gifts, now's the time to speak up, because we've got another 10 days of this." And I said, "No, no, just curious. And I don't want to spoil the flow, because I heard that in just a few days, I'm getting five gold rings." And my true love said to me, "Yeah, about that. You may have misheard. What I really got you is five goldspinks—a goldspink is another kind of bird."

And I said, "My true love, I have to admit, I don't even know what's going on here. You're giving me all these birds; you're repeating gifts day after day. And what does it even mean that there are

12 days of Christmas? Christmas is just one day. And if we keep it up like this with all the gifts, that means that by the end of 12 days, I'm going to have 364 gifts total." And my true love said to me, "It's actually a pretty interesting story. It's lost on most of us today, even though everyone hears the song every year. You should look into it." And so we shall.

Twelve Days, You Say

Nowadays, we think of the Christmas season as the festive time leading up to Christmas, usually starting more or less officially the day after Thanksgiving. But traditionally, the time leading up to Christmas is recognized as the Advent season, and for much of its history, it was a time of restraint and religious devotion. The period from Christmas Day to the eve of Epiphany was the official Christmas season, with festivities lasting for 12 days and ending on what's known as Twelfth Night which, as you may know, is also the title of a Shakespeare play. He was believed to have written it specifically to be played as Twelfth Night entertainment to close out the Christmas season.

As for the song "The Twelve Days of Christmas," let's go back to the beginning. "The text was printed without the music first, according to our earliest records, in 1780," says Mark Sundram, language professor at Laurentian University in Canada.

One big reason it first appeared without music is that it was never intended to be a song in the first place. After all, most Christmas carols from that era would include some kind of religious reference. The first time it showed up in print was in a children's book titled *Mirth without Mischief*, but as for how long the lyrics may have existed before they first appeared in print, nobody's sure.

Try to Remember

"It seems to have originally been a game," notes Sundram. "It's not the sort of carol that we think of today. It doesn't particularly refer to any religious topic; instead, it seems to be a kind of out-growth of this idea that during the Christmas season, there would be revelry and games and celebration. And in this particular game, with each verse, you add another item to an ever-growing list and see if you can remember the whole list as you get into more and more items. And if you flub something, then you lose the game."

This kind of elimination-style game is what's known as a "forfeit game." The published lyrics, if you can even call them that, would go on to be set to music—according to Sundram, the melody was an adaptation of a pre-existing folk tune—and that happened in 1909 by an English composer named Frederic Austin.

Some have argued that the song really does include religious references; it's just that they're veiled. For example, the three French hens represent the three theological virtues of faith, hope, and charity. But the simple truth is that this is just some convenient theory that has shown up in very recent history, with no basis in historical record at all. Besides, there are more than two dozen published versions of the song with significant variations among them. In one version, for example, the gift giver is not "my true love," but rather "my mother." In another, the pear tree is replaced with a juniper tree. There have been ducks a-quacking and lambs a-bleating and all kinds of other gifts over the centuries.

Sometimes a Pear Tree Isn't a Pear Tree

So if the items aren't secret religious symbols, then what are they? Sometimes the simplest answer is the best one. There's no reason to think they're anything other than the kinds of things that would appear in a children's game or be published in a children's book at that time. But that doesn't mean we can't still do some exploring. As Sundram elaborates, "The Latin word for 'partridge' was 'perdix.' It goes back to an Indo-European root, which means 'to fart.' The bird probably got its name because the distinctive sound that its wings make when flapping resemble another sound we're all familiar with.

"And in fact, 'fart' is the only cognate-related word in English to 'partridge.' And 'perdix' produced the French word 'perdrix,' which sounds a bit like 'pear tree.' And so, someone along the way might have got confused and reanalyzed that French word as 'pear tree.'"

And what about the turtle doves? "Well, the funny thing is that the turtle originally wasn't a turtle," Sundram continues. "The word 'turtle' existed first to refer to what we now think of as the turtle dove. And the word 'turtle' on its own, historically, was just used to refer to that bird. Basically, it's imitative of the sound of the bird, the sort of cooing that we associate with the dove."

May I Say Who's Calling?

And those calling birds aren't actually calling—that's just a misheard and reinterpreted version of the original lyric, which had them as "colly birds," or literally, coal-y birds, as in coal-colored birds.

In other words, blackbirds. And as you've already heard, those five gold rings may be another example of the original lyric being misheard. It may refer to goldspinks, another name for gold-finches, or it may refer to the rings around the necks of pheasants. Either way, it was likely keeping with the bird motif of days one through four. On days six through nine, we have pipers piping and drummers drumming and so on. In other words, it breaks out from the bird motif and shifts to human characters.

"It may just be a question that originally the game was shorter, and it was just the birds," Sundram theorizes, "and then someone added to the list a bunch of other things."

PART IV

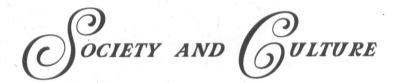

SOCIETY AND CULTURE

Society influences Christmas, which in turn influences society. Everything from consumer habits, to the language we use, to some of our most recently formed traditions are part of this constant feedback loop. Why do we say "Merry Christmas"? How did the rapid rise of print media and industrialization shape the holiday? And what might the current cultural conditions tell us about where Christmas is heading?

CHAPTER 23

CHRISTMAS ADVERTISING

Shaping the Season, One Sales Pitch at a Time

For as long as Christmas has been a major shopping holiday, merchants and service providers have vied for our attention and a share of our Christmas spending budget. And it's no coincidence that Christmas started to become a major shopping holiday in the 18th century, around the same time that mass print media was coming into its own.

This new ability to communicate on a massive scale not only helped to socialize the very idea of Christmas in America, but it also created new opportunities for sellers to reach potential buyers, and to link Christmas and commerce.

You'll Go Down in (Retail) History

The history of Christmas advertising permeates the season, from Coca-Cola creating—or at least perfecting—the modern image of Santa Claus (see Chapter 9), to the way Rudolph the Red-Nosed Reindeer (see Chapter 13) started out as a promotional giveaway for the Montgomery Ward department store.

You may wince at the idea that advertising is a proper Christmas tradition, but its role in shaping the season is undeniable. Seasonal ads have become as much a part of the atmosphere of the season as your favorite carols. You may even feel a pang of nostalgia when coming across a Christmas ad from your childhood.

For better or worse, Christmas advertising is part of the season, and it's here to stay. How it got to today's scale is the result of a web of economic, cultural, and technological forces coming together around the same time.

Hear Ye, Hear Ye

Arguably, one of the first uses of mass print media aimed at Christmas spending came in the form of the "carrier's address." These were printed sheets delivered by newspaper boys to their customers, containing a verse requesting a Christmas gratuity, in the form of a tip.

Carrier's addresses were essentially wassailing (see Chapter 6) in print form. The practice began in Philadelphia in the 1730s and was common a few decades later in Boston.

A Carrier's Address from Boston, 1771

The Lad Who Carries the Massachusetts Spy *wishes all his kind customers a A Merry Christmas and a Happy New Year! And presents the following:*

May grateful omens now appear,
To make the New a happy Year,
And bless th'esuing days:
May future peace in every mind,
Like odours wafted by the wind,
Its sweetest incense raife.

May George in his extensive reign,
Subdue the pride of haughty Spain
Submissive to its feet.
Thy princely smiles our ills appease;
Then grant that harmony and peace
The dawning year may greet.

Kind sirs! your gen'rous bounty show,
Few shillings on your Lad bestow,
Which will reward his pains,
Who piercing Winter's cold endures,
And to your hands the SPY secures
And still his task maintains

The practice must have been effective, because soon lamplighters, blacksmith's apprentices, and watchmen adopted the idea. Of course these don't qualify as proper advertisements, only as a connection between print media and Christmas spending.

Read It in the Sunday Papers

Christmas print ads as we might recognize them today began in England in the 18th century.

Toward the later decades of the century, similar ads appeared in American publications, but things really took off toward the later part of the 19th century. After a depression in the 1870s, America entered a booming period of prosperity, fueled by a near doubling of industrial production. And right around this time, American print media was exploding. Between 1880 and 1900, the number of daily newspapers in America went from 917 to 2,226. By 1900, America was publishing more than half the newspapers in the world.

By the 1890s, Christmas ads were a nationwide phenomenon, fueled in part by the fact that some periodicals were circulating nationwide. This was all new, and it gave advertisers a much wider reach.

In the late 19th century, trade cards were a common form of Christmas advertising. These were typically 4 x 6 cards, either handed out in shops or placed inside product packaging. Trade cards featured original artwork, printed in full color.

All of this was a potent mix of the right conditions to turn Christmas into a major shopping and advertising event. During this time, wrapping paper (see Chapter 17), store-bought gifts, and Christmas trees were newly becoming a normal part of the Christmas season.

In general, the nation's manufacturers were producing more goods than we could consume, so there was a shift toward developing new markets for selling them. This would involve coming up with novel ways of cultivating desire.

Cathedrals of Commerce

According to Penne L. Restad, the author of *Christmas in America: A History* and an American history lecturer at the University of Texas, "The development of the department store becomes important. One of the first ones is Wanamaker's in Philadelphia, but also Fields in Chicago and other stores. They're built on a model of a cathedral. So if you go into Wanamaker's—even now you walk into it, it's now a Macy's—you look up, and it goes up; the atrium is quite high. There's this huge pipe organ on the second floor, and the idea was to get women to come into this space. And there are all sorts of glass cabinets and good lighting—it just kind of presented things as being beautiful."

By the late 19th century, there was a growing middle class. Printing was very inexpensive, and manufacturing capabilities had skyrocketed. It was the perfect mix of conditions for advertising in general, and for Christmas in particular, to take off. And these things have a way of taking on a life of their own. For example, due to increased advertising in manufacturing, more people were buying toys. The demand was so high that more and more toy stores started to pop up, which of course would rely on Christmas sales to stay afloat, which in turn meant they'd advertise at Christmas.

The Birth of Window Shopping

Merchants would also create storefront displays to attract attention from passersby. Macy's in New York has had a special Christmas window since it opened in 1858.

The plateglass store display would forever change Christmas. Here, we see children gazing into a Macy's window in New York City, circa 1908. LIBRARY OF CONGRESS

From Plateglass Windows to Microsoft Windows

"The eye has to travel," noted the legendary fashion editor Diana Vreeland, and Penne Restad *observes that each innovation in advertising, from the in-person department store window to the online computer screen, involves a learning curve where the observer recalibrates the way they see the world.*

"First, you've got to invent the window, which is part of the idea of creating the department store–as-cathedral. Technology gets to be good enough that you can have a big enough window, and you can put in electricity, so now you can light the window. Now it can go after dark. You can't reach into it, but you can look at all these things.

"Originally, these windows were just filled with stuff. And as window dressing comes along, it becomes more of a design task. You would focus people's attention on this dress and all the things that went with the dress, rather than your eye being just bombarded. Remember the first web pages? Where you didn't know where to look? And then web designers started to figure out how to get people to read four corners of a web page simultaneously. Our eyes had to be trained in some way, but as our eyes are being trained, the web designers were also learning how to work with the sense of expectation. We look in particular places, so we're really working back and forth with web designers for that whole user experience.

"This is something that happens with department-store windows as well. They learn to put all the teapots in one place, and all the dresses are red dresses. Then the next thing that starts to happen is, of course at Christmas time, here comes the competition, just thinking of the famous walkways down going down Fifth Avenue. Once this store starts to create this sort of a tableau, then the next store decides to put moving parts in theirs. And so that becomes a whole art in itself."

"Now that passerby going down Fifth Avenue in New York City goes, 'Oh, look at that,' and you can't touch things," says Restad. "But it does create this world of fantasy and desire that is out of reach. I'm really keen on this idea of advertisers creating desire, so it's not necessarily having the thing, but it's that anticipation, which is also what Christmas is." None of this would have been possible if it weren't for the widespread availability of plateglass starting in the 19th century. Displays at stores like Macy's and Wanamaker's attracted people by the hundreds of thousands, as stores competed to outdo each other.

Five Beloved U.S. Christmas TV Spots

While Christmas advertising on television takes on different flavors around the world—department stores in the United Kingdom go all-out with TV spots that play more like mini-movies—certain television commercials in the United States have themselves become indispensable parts of the holiday season.

1. *Norelco Shavers—The stop-motion-animated image of Santa Claus riding a Norelco shaver across a snowy landscape (and the changing of the brand name to "Noëlco" to facilitate the tagline "Even our name says Merry Christmas") dates back to 1961, but the company has periodically tweaked and updated it up to the present day.*

2. *Hershey's Kisses—A pyramid of ten Kisses as "bells," playing a handbell-choir version of "We Wish You a Merry Christmas," debuted in 1989. Its popularity was underscored by a 2020 controversy, in which the company released a new version of the ad, featuring a young girl grabbing and eating one of the Kisses midperformance. Online commenters were furious, and the revised ad did not return the following year.*

3. *Fruity Pebbles—Post launched Fruity Pebbles and Cocoa Pebbles in 1971, named after the daughter on* The Flintstones, *and featuring ads with Fred Flintstone constantly having his cereal stolen by neighbor and best friend Barney Rubble. In the 1995 Christmas version of the ads, Santa Claus convinces Fred that it's the season of sharing. The commercial is scored to a version of "Deck the Halls," with Barney singing the immortal line, "Ho-ho-ho, I'm hu-hu-hungry."*

4. *André Sparkling Wine—Constant repetition of this commercial during the 1970s made most Generation Xers associate the tune of "Carol of the Bells" with clinking glasses and the consumption of Cold Duck (a mix of red wine and sparkling wine).*

5. *Coca-Cola—Having already had a hand in the design (and commodification) of Santa Claus (see Chapter 9), the Coca-Cola Company maintained its Christmastime presence with two ad campaigns that have popped up over and over throughout the years—one involving adorable polar bears, the other featuring the big red 18-wheeler Coca-Cola trucks, lighting up a town to the tune of Melanie Thornton's "Wonderful Dream (Holidays Are Coming)."*

CHAPTER 24

WHY DO WE SAY "MERRY CHRISTMAS"?

Maybe It's Because We Like to Party

"Happy Christmas."

It sounds weird, doesn't it? Maybe a little pretentious, at least when an American tries to say it. Here in America, we wish one another a "Merry Christmas." And just as importantly, we don't wish one another a "merry" one of anything else. In fact, with just a few unremarkable exceptions, the word "merry" nowadays seems to be reserved almost exclusively for spreading holiday cheer.

Why? Well, it's a combination of language changing over time, a bit of influence from the printing and publishing industries. and the story of a phrase that survived a Victorian crackdown on partying in the streets.

To Your Health

"Happy" and "Merry" may sound interchangeable, and to some extent, they are: Both refer to a pleasant or joyous state of mind, but there is a subtle distinction that makes all the difference.

Linguist Arika Okrent writes about language, and she's the author of *In the Land of Invented Languages.* "'Merry' is the older word, the one that's been in English for longer," she says. "It's more a sense of cheerfulness; it comes from the same root that gave rise to the word 'mirth.' It used to be more widely applied, so you could say something like, 'Oh, merry weather we're having today.'"

The iconic Currier & Ives lithograph (1876). LIBRARY OF CONGRESS

"For centuries, both 'Merry Christmas' and 'Happy Christmas' were used as a way to wish someone a good holiday. But over time, ['merry'] became more associated with toasting and carousing and drinking and getting a little bit rowdy."

So while "happy" and "merry" do have a lot in common, the difference is that, over time, "merry" suggested a more active expression of happiness—"to make merry"—while "happy," on the other hand, was more passive, and arguably more sober and sedate. (Remember that point; we're going to come back to it soon.)

An active expression of happiness was a perfect thing to associate with Christmas, and so the phrase "Merry Christmas" was born.

For a good stretch, "Happy Christmas" and "Merry Christmas" peacefully coexisted—until the 19th century. On this side of the Atlantic in 1823, a professor named Clement Clarke Moore published a poem titled "A Visit from St. Nicholas." When it was originally published in a New York newspaper on Christmas Eve, the final line of the poem read, "But I heard him exclaim, ere he drove out of sight, 'Happy Christmas to all, and to all a good night!'"

Twenty years later, in England, Charles Dickens would publish *A Christmas Carol*, and in the opening scene, Scrooge's nephew bursts into the counting house to say, "A Merry Christmas, uncle! God save you." Of course, *A Christmas Carol* was a best seller, which helped to further popularize "Merry," and so did something else that happened that same year—the first commercially printed Christmas cards.

Those first Christmas cards (see Chapter 25) displayed the message, "A Merry Christmas and a Happy New Year to you." "Merry" became associated with the Victorian ideal of Christmas, which was hugely influential on how Americans celebrate the holiday. So it wasn't long before "Merry Christmas" caught on here in America, to the point where later publications of "A Visit from St. Nicholas" usually changed the final line to, "But I heard him exclaim, ere he drove out of sight, 'Merry Christmas to all, and to all a good night!'"

Did You Know?

Someone had to be the first to say it . . . or write it, as the case may be. The first known example of "Merry Christmas" appeared in a letter from the 16th century. In it, a bishop writing to England's Chief Minister expressed his wish for God to send him a merry Christmas.

The 16th century also gave us the song "God Rest Ye Merry, Gentlemen," which further solidified the association between "Merry" and Christmas.

C'mon, Get "Happy"

But back in England, it wasn't just Dickens and Christmas cards that were influencing how people thought of Christmas. Christmas celebrations before the 19th century were very different from what we know today. They would involve carolers going door to door, people celebrating and drinking in the streets, getting loud and quite often rowdy, and even violent, and the problem only got worse as more people moved to cities for factory jobs.

So there was something of a culture shift, starting with the upper classes who wanted to rebrand Christmas as more of a family-centered domestic celebration than a public one. Given that "Merry" implied an active role and festivity, the upper classes decided it was time to move away from wishing people a "Merry" Christmas and wish them a "Happy" one instead.

According to Okrent, "It was considered a little more classy to say 'Happy Christmas.' 'Merry,' one person put it, had a 'ridiculous, excessive sentiment to it.' It was a little bit too over-the-top as a greeting."

This trend continued for several decades; "Happy Christmas" was now the highbrow expression. King George V used it in the first Royal Christmas radio address in 1932: "To all, to each, I wish a Happy Christmas. God bless you."

But here in America, "Merry Christmas" has stuck, even as the word "merry" itself was falling out of general use and starting to disappear.

But What about England?

"They do still say both in England, 'Merry Christmas' and 'Happy Christmas,'" says linguist Arika Okrent. "But lots of people there insist that they never say 'Happy Christmas,' they only say 'Merry Christmas.'

"You can hear in the Royal Address that they say 'Happy Christmas.' In the Harry Potter movies, they say 'Happy Christmas.' It's almost like they don't even notice that they do say 'Happy Christmas.' But certainly when Americans think of what British people do, there's the thought that 'Oh, this sounds really different, and a little bit exotic and very British somehow.' But a lot of British people insist they don't say it anymore, although you can find a lot of evidence that they do."

Think about it: Today, we have "Merry Christmas," merry-go-rounds, and the phrase "the more the merrier." Other than that, and the occasional person named Meredith who goes by Merry, you don't really hear the word anymore. It's what Okrent calls a "fossilized word." "['Merry Christmas'] is so entrenched in ritual activity—not just religious rituals, but all kinds of rituals surrounding what we do, how we greet each other, the songs we sing, the cards we send. It's all very strongly bound up with this phrase."

CHAPTER 25

CHRISTMAS IN THE MAIL

Special Deliveries

Our modern Christmas celebration relies on a well-functioning postal system. Nowadays, the US Postal Service delivers more than 15 billion packages, cards, and letters during the Christmas season. Whether it's friends and families staying connected through Christmas card exchanges, or children writing their letters to the North Pole, the daily deliveries from mail carriers are a vital part of the season.

After all, it just wouldn't be Christmas without all those Christmas cards that end up lining the mantel or taped around the doorway.

Have you ever stopped to wonder how Christmas cards came to be the annual tradition they are? It's a story of many historic and economic and technological developments all coming together around the same time. And just like it is with a lot of the Christmas traditions we celebrate today, this one's relatively new.

The very practice of exchanging written greetings traces all the way back to ancient Egypt. But the Christmas card itself comes to us from England. Around the 1800s, Valentines were already very popular. These were ornate handmade pieces, and they were usually delivered in person.

According to Stephanie Boydell, curator at Manchester Metropolitan University Special Collections, Christmas cards "come out of the idea of leaving your *carte de visite*—you would drop by to somebody's house, and you'd have a little card that would have your name on it and your title. So the first cards were basically personalized cartes de visite." Manchester Metropolitan University Special Collections' Laura Seddon Greeting Card Collection houses a collection of over 100,000 greeting cards, including one of the few remaining originals of the first commercially produced Christmas card.

Put a Stamp on It

Delivering them by hand was the custom, but it was also true that sending them through the mail just wasn't really a good option. The postal system back then was disjointed and unreliable, and the rate varied wildly. But all of that changed in 1840, when the UK introduced the uniform Penny Post. This created the idea of a postage stamp, where for a standardized price—just a penny at the time, hence the name—anyone could send a letter anywhere in the UK.

The first commercially printed Christmas card, 1843. WIKIMEDIA COMMONS

This was huge. There was no Internet back then, of course, no telephones, no automobiles. Communicating across long distances just wasn't part of normal life for most people. And then, just like that, it became cheap and reliable and efficient. This was also a time of rising education and literacy in Great Britain. Literacy rates had been fairly flat since the mid-17th century, but they took off like a rocket during the 19th century. More people could read and write, which meant more letters in the mail.

Economic prosperity and consumerism were also on the rise. And just a couple of decades before, a new printing technique known as lithography had made mass printing production cheaper and more efficient, and it was catching on. So all of the conditions were in place for someone to come up with the idea of mass-producing greeting cards to be sent at Christmastime. And in 1843, a man named Henry Cole did just that. "He produced it initially as a personal card for sending out, but then produced many more," says Boydell.

A Tradition Is Born

It was almost inevitable for a man like Cole—he was also one of the people behind the Penny Post, and he's often credited with designing the very first postage stamp. So he commissioned an artist named John Calcott Horsley to design a greeting card. The Cole-Horsley card, as it's sometimes known, sold for a shilling, and he produced about 2,000 of them. It was what we'd now call a postcard, meaning it was printed on one side, and it didn't fold in half.

The design shows a large Victorian family, each member raising a glass of wine and a toast to the recipient. And in front of them is a banner reading "A Merry Christmas and a Happy New Year to You." In the early days, Christmas cards didn't look very much like the ones we're all used to today. The designs were mainly floral patterns or springtime scenes.

"And there are other cards which look more like fashion plates," recounts Boydell. "All it's got is a woman in a pleasant dress with a parasol, taking a stroll outside, and it says 'A Happy Christmas.' It's a most un-Christmasy scene."

And the ones that did show Christmas celebrations were sometimes pretty silly. Notes Boydell, "There's a whole series of cards, which show you traditional dinner coming back at you. A Christmas pudding with legs, for instance, or the turkey with a knife, chasing people, trying to capture them and eat them instead."

But boy, did they catch on. They became so popular that some editorials even complained that more important mail couldn't be delivered because of all the Christmas cards overloading the postal system. Postmasters even recommended mailing them early.

Fine Art, in Your Mailbox

It didn't take long for Christmas cards to cross the Atlantic. In 1875, a printer named Louis Prang began selling Christmas cards in America. Just a few years later, his business was printing over five million cards a year. Prang would hire well-known artists to create designs for his cards, which became part of their selling point. It's even been said that through his Christmas cards, Louis Prang introduced fine art to the average person who, in 1875, had probably never spent much time in an art museum.

Ultimately, poor Louis Prang became a victim of his own success. When cheap imitations flooded the market, it drove him out of business.

When Santa Brings Your Letter

Two key reforms to the US Postal Service were instrumental in making it part of Christmas.

The Rural Free Delivery program of the late nineteenth century established mail delivery directly to rural destinations. Previously, home delivery and pickup in these locations did not happen, and people living there would need to pick up mail themselves at the post office.

"It made sending and receiving mail more accessible to more people, and created new opportunities for personal connections," says Alex Palmer, author of The Atlas of Christmas and The Santa Claus Man. "And some early descriptions of this new service referred to Santa Claus, because the experience felt so magical."

In 1913, the Postal Service introduced the parcel post: the ability to send packages in the mail. "When they passed the parcel post, it totally opened up the floodgates for gifts," says Palmer. "In 1913, the number of gifts being sent in the mail was two to three times higher than it had been in 1912."

Wishing You Were Home

Most Christmas cards were still postcards at this point. But in 1914, an American named J. C. Hall saw the potential for greeting cards mailed in envelopes, and things ended up going very well for him and his company, Hallmark Cards. Around this time, airmail was taking off (no pun intended) and demand was booming for cards to be sent to all of those soldiers serving in World War I. In fact, the First and Second World Wars were really instrumental in driving demand for Christmas cards, which eventually led to them being part of the normal Christmas season for all of us.

Americans love sending greeting cards, but the numbers are on the decline. The latest figures show that the average American household receives about 20 Christmas cards in a given year, down almost 50% from only 30 years ago.

Sending Letters to Santa

You might be surprised to learn that before children started writing to Santa, he was writing to them. "The correspondence is not from kids to Santa, but from Santa to children, reminding them to be good kids for the year," according to Nancy Pope, the head curator at the National Postal Museum in Washington, DC. It's part of the Smithsonian Institution. "So, you know, Santa wants to make sure that you're behaving, and you're doing what you need to do. It was a 'Look out, or . . .' type of thing."

Evidently, many parents wrote letters to their children in the voice of Santa to comment on their behavior, and to remind them how Santa treats children who don't behave themselves. Well, it wasn't long before children got the idea that they could write back. In the 1870s, some post offices around the country were receiving letters addressed to Santa, "and there were newspapers that started talking about Santa and saying there was an address," says Pope. "Santaclausville, North Pole" shows up after the Civil War as an address for Santa.

Thomas Nast—one of the key architects of the modern portrayal of Santa Claus (see Chapter 9)—drew a cartoon for Harper's Weekly in 1871, showing St. Nick dividing his correspondence between "Good Children's Parents" and "Naughty Children's Parents," cementing the idea of Santa as someone who reads his mail and responds accordingly.

With the coming of the 20th century and beyond, many children's letters to Santa wound up in the Dead Letter Office, with a few generous souls stepping in to try to fulfill the wishes of young boys and girls. Such efforts have led to crime—a legendary con man named John Gluck launched an elaborate scam in 1913 with his Santa Claus Association—and genuine philanthropy, as postal workers launched a program called Operation Santa Claus in 1912, making Christmas dreams come true to this day.

THE SATURDAY EVENING POST

An Illustrated Weekly
Founded A.D. 1728 by Benj. Franklin

DEC. 9, 1922

5c. THE COPY
10c. in Canada

Alice Duer Miller—Joseph Hergesheimer—George Pattullo—Captain Dingle

CHAPTER 26

THE FUTURE OF CHRISTMAS PAST

Will These Current Trends Change Christmas?

Christmas comes once a year, and never the same way twice. Each Christmas season, we collectively write the next chapter in a never-ending story. It happens in ways large and small. The last 20 years have brought a sea change in our Christmas buying habits as online shopping became the norm. Those same 20 years have also seen a growing sentiment among many Americans that there is an ongoing "war on Christmas." (A 2021 survey found that 37% of Americans hold this belief.) And in the last few years, critics and fans have been calling out the classic song "Baby, It's Cold Outside" for its lyrics being out of step with modern attitudes.

So it goes, season after season, the ebb and flow of things added to Christmas and things removed, things that will endure (like the electric Christmas lights invented in the 1880s) and things will quickly fade (like the aluminum Christmas trees of the 1960s). These changes reflect current fashions, social change, economic conditions, and the massive presence of the retail and entertainment industries. Though these changes seem small or even imperceptible from one season to the next, they have a cumulative effect over time.

What this means is that at any given point in history, we're witnessing not only certain traditions in decline, but also the trends that just may become lasting additions to Christmas. (Or, dare we use that contradiction in terms, "new traditions"?)

When it comes to traditions in decline, we can look at the obvious fads that came and went, and also at our general attitudes toward certain traditions. In 2013, Pew Research Center published a report titled "Celebrating Christmas and the Holidays, Then and Now." The report, based on a survey of 2,000 American adults, shed light on how the respondents celebrate Christmas as adults, compared to what their celebrations were typically like when they were growing up. While 69% said they attended a Christmas church service growing up, only 54% planned to in 2013. There were similar declines in activities like sending Christmas cards, exchanging homemade gifts, and going caroling. Surprisingly, putting up a Christmas tree saw double-digit decline, from 92% to 79%.

Will the day come in some far-off future when caroling is all but extinct, and the Christmas tree is no longer the main Christmas decoration in the home? Almost certainly, just as the day came when the Christmas tree replaced mistletoe and holly as the main Christmas decoration, or when serving a boar's head for Christmas dinner became an historical relic.

As for the current trends that will go on to become the traditions of future generations, of course we can only confirm these things in hindsight. But there's no harm in speculating. Here are six of the strongest contenders from the last decade that just may make a lasting change to Christmas as we know it.

Ugly Christmas Sweaters

The Nordic-inspired Christmas sweaters of the 1950s and 60s were out of style by the 1970s. But they were given new life in the 2010s when people began rescuing them from thrift stores and attic storage boxes to wear to ironic "ugly sweater parties." What began as a local phenomenon in Vancouver, British Columbia, quickly caught fire, helped along by the rise of social media. Soon, ugly sweaters (or "Christmas jumpers" in the UK) became a ubiquitous addition to the season, as well as a multimillion-dollar industry. Each season brings a new line of intentionally ugly, gaudy, tacky Christmas sweaters, often featuring edgy humor. Recent years have brought designs sponsored by celebrities and major brands.

Is the ugly sweater a fad or a lasting addition to Christmas? Given that they've already survived more than a decade, and continue to be a growing industry, it doesn't look like they're going away soon. They've worked their way into popular culture. You can even buy ugly sweater coloring books, cookie decorating kits, and T-shirts made to resemble an ugly sweater.

The ugly sweater may also have started a trend toward other forms of Christmas attire. Since the mid-2010s, "fam jams" (matching pajama sets meant for families to wear on Christmas morning) have been gaining popularity. They, too, have become big business, and are likely here with us for the foreseeable future.

In addition to being a fun and festive part of the Christmas scenery, ugly sweaters and fam jams are appropriate attire for curling up on the sofa to partake in another trend . . .

Made-for-TV Christmas Romance Movies

Made-for-TV Christmas movies are nothing new. Nor is the concept of a romance story set against the backdrop of the Christmas season. But since the 2010s, TV Christmas romances have become a major phenomenon. Formulaic, conspicuously wholesome, and filled with tropes and absurd plot holes, these movies have nonetheless earned a devoted fan base. And with several dozen new ones arriving each year, those fans could watch a new movie every day of the Christmas season, and still have plenty left over. Hallmark alone (the biggest player in this space) produced 41 new Christmas romances in 2021 between the Hallmark Channel and Hallmark Movies & Mysteries.

TV Christmas romances have reshaped the world of Christmas entertainment by setting a new standard for the kinds of stories we most closely associate with Christmas, and the way we want them told. At various times in the past, Christmas stories may have been ghost stories (*Between the Lights*), tragedies (*The Little Match Girl*), stories of homecomings (*As the Yule Log Burns*), or of class structure and personal redemption (*A Christmas Carol*). Will the 21st century be remembered as the era of Christmas stories about hometown hunks and small-town Christmases?

Whatever the future holds, it's clear that, as of the 2020s, we are in a golden age for Christmas TV romances. Hallmark's closest competitors like Lifetime, UPtv, and streaming services like Netflix are angling for their share of the market. In that way, they have also changed Christmas entertainment by setting expectations for a flood of new content each season.

If there's a limit to our appetite for this form of entertainment, we haven't reached it yet. And audiences aren't even necessarily waiting until the "official" Christmas season to tune in. Hallmark airs new Christmas movies beginning in October, and airs reruns year-round, which is part of yet another trend . . .

Extending the Christmas Season

The Christmas season seems to arrive earlier every year. Barely before the Halloween candy is off the shelves (or sometimes even earlier than that), Christmas items are spotted in stores. The common objection to so-called Christmas creep typically goes something like this: "Can't this wait until after Thanksgiving?" That sentiment reflects the widely held idea that the Christmas season "officially" starts on the Friday after the fourth Thursday of the month. But that too is a new notion, which, when introduced in the early 20th century, met similar criticism. The push to start the Christmas season earlier and earlier is largely driven by financial incentives for retailers and broadcasters. But it's also getting some help from Christmas enthusiasts who welcome the early arrival, and who are able to find validation and community online.

Are we witnessing a shift toward an extended Christmas season of up to eight weeks (or more), to replace our typical five? Recently, a growing number of people have embraced the idea of the "Ber Months," (referring to all of the months ending in "b-e-r") as an extended Christmas season.

If the Christmas season does become extended, then one character in particular will find himself working overtime . . .

The Elf on the Shelf

It may be difficult to imagine a proper Christmas tradition that relies on a single product produced by a private company. In 2005, Carol Aebersold and Chanda Bell published a children's picture book and accompanying figure of a "scout elf." The story tells of how scout elves hide in people's homes during the Christmas season to report children's behavior to the North Pole.

The Elf on the Shelf quickly became a must-have for families with small children. In the years after its debut, it became trendy to post pictures on social media of the elf in humorous situations. It has its own balloon in the Macy's Thanksgiving Day Parade, a breakfast cereal, several animated specials, spin-off merchandise, and a live musical stage production.

Fads and trends that reach these proportions are nothing new. The Cabbage Patch Kids of the 1980s followed a similar trajectory, for example. But what may be different about the Elf on the Shelf is that it's exclusively a Christmas item. By now, there is an entire generation that grew up never knowing a Christmas without the Elf on the Shelf. Will they continue the tradition in the next couple of decades as they start their own families?

Christmas Eve Boxes

Many families make a tradition of opening a gift on Christmas Eve, a sort of "pre-game" leading to the next morning's main event. Since the mid-2010s, the "Christmas Eve box" has taken that concept to the next level. The premise of the Christmas Eve box is that it's filled with small but meaningful items perfect for giving a child on Christmas Eve, things like festive pajamas, Christmas books, and sweets.

The trend has been quickly growing in the UK for years and, more recently, in America. Also known as a "Santa Claus box," they've recently become popular for giving to adults as well, or for creating one for the entire family.

The concept is somewhere between a stocking and a gift under the tree. It's a Christmas care package, meant to kick off the gift-giving festivities in a unique and special way. It's still too early to tell if the Christmas Eve box will gain long-term traction. But, as Christmas is a gift-giving holiday, it's easy to imagine the idea catching on.

What began as a small trend just a few years ago has quickly become a major and growing phenomenon, spurred mostly by social media. Retailers have taken note, too, and are looking for a piece of the action. We can expect more products in the coming years, which will push Christmas Eve boxes further into the mainstream.

Telepresence

When rail travel became common in the 19th century, it changed Christmas dramatically and permanently. The very notion of Christmas as a time for family reunions owes a lot to the availability of rail travel. Previously, Christmas travel was infrequent in areas where snow shut down the roads for long stretches. Suddenly, people could return from the city to their hometowns, and boarding-school children could come home for the holidays. Not only that, but large deliveries of food and other goods to cities were also possible, and raw materials could get to the factories that turned out the consumer goods that became Christmas gifts. The entire landscape of Christmas changed and, with it, so did our expectations and behaviors around Christmas.

The past century and a half have seen many new technologies that directly or indirectly influence our Christmas celebration, whether it's the telephone, car travel, air travel, television, movies, online shopping, and much more.

The period since the early 2020s suggests that another such change is upon us. Tools like Skype have been around for nearly 20 years, fulfilling that Jetsons-like promise of widespread video calling. But it was the effects of the COVID-19 pandemic that made video calls part of daily life for most people. Suddenly, even the most technophobic among us was mastering the intricacies of Zoom and FaceTime to stay connected in a world suddenly gone hostile toward in-person connections.

Much of this spilled over into the Christmas season. Children visited Santa Claus by video call. Popular Christmas shows, festivals, and markets made virtual offerings. Families spent Christmas morning gathered around a phone or tablet from separate houses. None of these things was new, but the pandemic was the tipping point that pushed them into the mainstream, and probably for good.

Nothing will ever replace a good old-fashioned family Christmas or attending a production of *The Nutcracker* in person. But our current technology has expanded our options at Christmastime, and will almost certainly continue to play a greater role in our Christmas culture.

ACKNOWLEDGMENTS

It takes a Christmas village to produce a book like this. Many thanks to my wonderful agent, Eric Myers, for saying "I think you've got something here," and for all his invaluable support and guidance throughout this process. Huge thanks to Alonso Duralde, author of *Have Yourself a Movie Little Christmas* and co-author of *I'll Be Home for Christmas Movies*, for being an indispensable creative partner in bringing *Christmas Past* from a podcast to the printed page. And thanks to everyone at Lyons Press, including Rick Rinehart and Diana Nuhn, for making this book the best it could be.

This book may not have existed without the early help and encouragement of Alex Palmer, author of *The Atlas of Christmas* and *The Santa Claus Man*. Thanks to Alex also for writing the wonderful foreword to this book. On a similar note, *Christmas Past*, the podcast, may not have existed without early help and encouragement from Lee Cameron. His podcast, *The Christmas Stocking*, is sorely missed and remains one of the best.

A big thanks to the entire *Christmas Past* audience ("hey, sugarplums!"), and a special shout-out to everyone who has ever recorded a Christmas memory to share on the show. Every season feels like an extended family gathering. I'm grateful for all the warm connections I've had with so many of you over the years.

Thanks to every subject matter expert who has been generous enough to appear on the podcast and share their expertise.

I'd also like to thank all my fellow independent Christmas creators, with special thanks to Tim Babb (*Can't Wait for Christmas*), Todd Killian (*Christmas Clatter*), Chantelle Joy Otto (*All Things Christmas*), Brandon Gray (*Deck the Hallmark*), Craig Newmark (*Weird Christmas*), Duane Bailey (*Tinsel Tunes*), and Glen Warren (*Seasons Eatings*). Your comradery and creative inspiration over the years have meant a lot.

Finally, I'd like to thank my mom, Donna Ewing, for instilling her Christmas spirit and creativity in me; my wife, Christine, for all of her love and support throughout this journey; and my son, Dashiell, for letting me relive Christmas through a child's eyes.

INDEX

ABOUT THE AUTHOR

Brian Earl is the host of *Christmas Past*, one of the longest-running podcasts about Christmas. He lives in California with his wife and son. Find out more at christmaspastpodcast.com.